The Other Side of Profc

The 'New Approaches to Care' series

Patients are people. They have feelings, families and fears. Whatever the cause for their seeking help, the caring professional will find that he or she will be concerned with these other issues. All illness carries with it anxiety and each person has very individual and important feelings about it; feelings which can easily be forgotten or neglected when nurses become preoccupied with the details of treatments, procedures and ward routines.

The *New Approaches to Care* series aims to explore this 'other side' of care in a practical and realistic way, emphasising the importance of meeting all the patients' needs, while recognising the constraints and problems which so often make the 'other side' the forgotten side of patient care.

The books in this series examine the implications that treatments, procedures, investigations and routines can have for patients and their families. They also aim to help nurses gain some insight into the problems, feelings and anxieties which people can experience when they are being looked after in hospital or the community. The series will thus offer a tangible starting point for all nurses and other professionals, both in training and in practice, to give their patients the most complete and understanding care possible.

Series Editors

June Jolly, SRN, RSCN, has devoted most of her nursing career to the care of sick children, and was involved with establishing a new paediatric unit at Brook General Hospital, Woolwich.

Jill Macleod Clark, BSc, PhD, SRN, is a Lecturer in the Department of Nursing Studies, Chelsea College, University of London.

Will Bridge, BSc, PhD, is the Co-ordinator of the Learning Resources Unit at Brighton Polytechnic.

Other titles in this series

Heaven's Very Special Child

A meeting was held quite far from earth
'It's time again for another birth'
Said the angels to the Lord above
'This special child will need much love

His progress may seem very slow
Accomplishments he may not show
And he'll require extra care
From the folks he meets down there

He may not run, or laugh or play
His thoughts may seem so far away
In many ways he won't adapt
And he'll be known as handicapped

So let's be careful where he's sent
We want his life to be content
Please Lord, find parents who
Will do a special job for you

They will not realise right away
The leading role they're asked to play
But with this child sent from above
Comes stronger faith and richer love

And soon they'll know the privilege given
In caring for this gift from Heaven
This precious child, so meek and mild
Is Heaven's Very Special Child.'

Anon.

For my friends in Harrow, all of whom are very special

THE OTHER SIDE OF PROFOUND HANDICAP

Pat Brudenell
RMN, RDTh, DipDTh, AIST, Cert Ed

Photographs by
John Crowson

Front Cover by
Gillian Simmonds

MACMILLAN

First published 1986

Published by
MACMILLAN EDUCATION LTD
Houndmills, Basingstoke, Hampshire RG21 2XS
and London
Companies and representatives
throughout the world

Typeset by TecSet Ltd,
Sutton, Surrey
Printed in Hong Kong

British Library Cataloguing in Publication Data
Brudenell, Pat
The other side of profound handicap.—(New
approaches to care)
1. Mentally handicapped—Care and treatment
I. Title   II. Series
362.3′8   HV3004
ISBN 0-333-40490-4
ISBN 0-333-41812-3 Pbk

Contents

Foreword

When asked to read the first draft of this book, I approached it with caution: having worked in the field of handicap for many years, was yet another expert going to tell us lesser mortals what to do? I was amply reassured. Pat Brudenell has brought together a book that explores *with us* the problems concerning profound mental handicap, rather than talking *at us*. Based on the author's own lengthy experience, we are guided through the important basic areas that all of us, professionals, parents and volunteers, need to address if we are to maximise our own potential and the potential of those with whom we work.

The book starts by putting the problems of mental handicap into a historical perspective from the Middle Ages until now, and pointing out the appalling conditions that so many disabled people had to live in, including total non-differentiation between themselves and people who were also mentally ill. The information on the legal aspects of handicap are clear and at times appalling: I had to remember that it was not until 1983 that the phrase 'educationally subnormal' was replaced by 'children with learning difficulties'. A very comprehensive section on the family deals realistically with so many issues besetting the family who have a handicapped child. The case histories are clear and helpful and point out how much more strain families of handicapped children have. There are various suggestions on helping with this, one of which I should mention: why must we all assume that the parents of a handicapped child *necessarily* want to spend all their spare time with other parents of handicapped children?

The book goes on to discuss the importance of professional staffing for Special Care Units. It is easy for this area to attract less qualified staff because it is so often considered the Cinderella of the professions. Untrained staff are not dismissed — they have a valuable part to play in a total care programme. But what about staff support? Pat Brudenell makes the strong plea that staff working under such demands and in Units that are so often very isolated need a very strong support system.

The material on assessment and recording of progress is well described and most useful. We are then introduced to very basic, clear ideas in play, movement, art and music. The practical examples are most appropriate and will give heart to the most jaded worker. Often staff forget that creative ideas do *work* and regard structured rote learning as the only approach to the education of handicapped people.

Pat Brudenell brings a wealth of ideas to this subject. Her own zest for living and working is apparent throughout the book. There are some delightful glimpses of the author herself. For example, she says: 'I have always had a bit of a soft spot for manic patients . . . . There is something quite splendid about feeling on top of the world.'

This book is both optimistic about mentally handicapped people in the 1980s and also realistic. No one will get false hope through this material. Rather I would describe it as creative realism with a lot of humanity! A pertinent example of the human side of the book is the somewhat chaste reminder to get out of our stereotyped ideas about presents we might buy for mentally handicapped people. Have we ever thought of 'buying a little luxury'?

I warmly recommend this book to all those working with profoundly handicapped people. I know they will find it both stimulating and supportive.

Hertfordshire, 1985   Sue Jennings, FRAI, RDTh,
Dip Soc Anthrop, LRAM, LGSM
Senior Lecturer and Course Leader
Hertfordshire College of Art and Design
and
Director, Dramatherapy Consultants

Preface

The 'New Approaches to Care' series looks at the other side of caring for a wide variety of people and patients of all ages. As part of the series, this book is primarily concerned with the care of the profoundly handicapped child and adult. Although much has been written about handicap, there has been very little written about profound mental handicap. Not having the benefits of being able to read about the experiences of others working in this field has made the task of developing new ideas all the more difficult. For myself, arriving at the point whereby I began to understand what profound handicap actually meant personally, enabled me to be far more receptive and resourceful in terms of what I was then able to do. If I can convey even a small part of this, then this book will have been worth while.

The idea stems from my own personal enjoyment and frustration of working in a Special Care Unit and with people with very special needs and is very much a personal statement. My rationale, interpretations and case studies are based upon my own experiences with my own groups. I have changed names and circumstances to protect the privacy and confidentiality that was entrusted to me. The views and attitudes expressed by parents are representative of those parents I interviewed. They may not be relevant to all family situations but they are nevertheless true of their own. I hope the reader will be able to relate to the various standpoints, as a parent, as a practitioner, as a friend or simply as an interested party.

I have deliberately kept off issues of benefits, equipment and theories as these areas and many more have been capably dealt with by other authors. There is little reference to specific diagnosis as I have tried to convey the entirety of handicap —

incorporating the whole person — bringing in aspects that go beyond the handicap itself.

Profoundly handicapped people are entirely dependent on others for all their needs. They can only rely on the voices of those around them to improve their quality of life, raise the standards of their care and protect their human and civil rights. The severity of their handicap prevents them from telling their own story. I only hope that my interpretations are somewhere near to their truth.

Harrow, 1985   P. B.

N. B. The views and opinions expressed in this book are personal to the author and are not reflective of the authority by whom she is employed.

Acknowledgements

Without the tremendous support and encouragement of so many people, this book would never have been written. My grateful thanks are given to all those who have knowingly and unknowingly contributed, but with special mention to the following:

To John Crowson for his patience in not only being able to capture a photographic record of my work but for his patience with me.

To friends and ex-colleagues — Sue, Jenny, Penny and Jenny. Their enthusiasm kept me going when the going got tough.

Special thanks to Pat Mickleburgh for her secretarial assistance and patience with the first draft.

To Sandi Hammond, for hours spent on the personal computer deciphering the final draft, but most especially for her tremendous support throughout the final stages. To her, my very special and heartfelt thanks.

To Printronic Corporation (UK) Ltd. I am indebted to the company for allowing me access to their technology, which assisted me enormously in the compilation of the final draft.

To friends who urged me to make a start, but especially to Jennifer. Her advice and guidance and share of the anguish and excitement of writing my first book tested friendship to the limits and beyond. To her, my very special thanks.

Mention must be made to the families I worked with and of course to their youngsters, who feature largely throughout the book. For allowing me the opportunity to see handicap from another angle and for teaching me so much, I am very grateful.

To Sue Jennings, for not only agreeing to write the fore-word but for being both tutor and friend. She has played a major role in my development as a therapist, and it was with her guidance and support that I was able to make the move to work with mentally handicapped people. For this and much more, my grateful thanks.

Finally to Robert. Throughout the chaos that this book has brought to our home, he has managed to hold onto his sense of humour and shared most of the traumas with a smile. To him, my very special thanks.

1 Looking at Handicap From All Sides

Looking at Society

INTRODUCTION

The people who care today and who will care tomorrow will determine the type of care that is provided for mentally handicapped children and adults. The trends to move from institution to community have given impetus to major changes in the field. Specialist professions have developed their skills towards new areas and more disciplines have become involved. Boundaries have become extended and developments and progress have been made. But profound handicap is still regarded as being the Cinderella of the caring professions. As so little is known and understood, there is still a tendency to regard the care for this group as being occupational rather than educational.

Services vary considerably, and one county's progress is another county's dream. If the subject area is one that is going to develop with purpose, then we need to look at the factors that are going to be instrumental in bringing this about. There is little to be gained from discussing the severity of handicap in isolation. To have some insight into what is really happening, we must be prepared to look at the part that we play in the process.

We can all probably recall some incident in the past when we were confronted with handicap for the first time. I am now ashamed to admit that, when I was a child, I hurriedly crossed the road to avoid having to walk past a young boy in a wheelchair. I needed to be able to put some distance between us. It did not occur to me then that this boy probably spent his entire life having people keep their distance from him.

The daughter of friends of my parents gave birth to a Down's syndrome child. Everyone seemed to care very much but nobody actually did anything constructive to help. The only way that anyone could deal with the situation was to ignore it. The child stayed with her parents, despite family and friends suggesting that 'it might be better if she went away'. The little girl suffered so much from being in the community, I wonder now if in fact it would not have been better had she been 'sent away'. The safety of an institution would have been far more secure than the environment the community offered her.

All that was over 20 years ago. It would be marvellous to think that the same thing couldn't happen today. The rationale then, though, was much the same as it is now. We tend to shut our eyes to things we find disturbing. When presented with a situation that is uncomfortable, we tend to sidestep the issue.

With growing technological advancement, there is a continuing improvement in diagnostic procedure. With increased media coverage, there is greater understanding of handicap within the community. But, despite the growth in these areas, there is still a widespread misunderstanding of handicap and an even greater misunderstanding of profound handicap. Handicap is not a new disease. It does not stop at a given age. It is not something that strikes and then goes away. It is here to stay. It is very, very final. It is one thing to acknowledge this finality, but quite another to do something about it.

By taking a long, hard look at what we are doing, by questioning our motives and purposes, we can arrive at a good base on which we can start to build. This book is very much concerned with attitudes; not just those of the people directly or indirectly involved with handicap but those of our society as a whole. In the past, much of what was decided was dealt with by people who knew very little about handicap. This is not so now. Or is it? People in positions of influence, with little experience and minimal, if any, contact

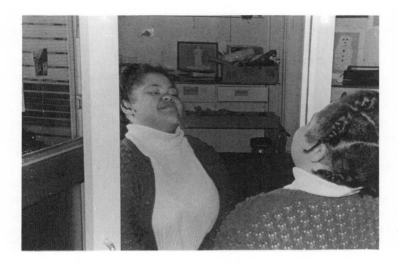

with handicap, hold power over resources of finance, equipment and staffing.

If we can arrive at a better understanding of what has gone on in the past, and by keeping up to date on current political and social moves, we can be better prepared for future planning and research.

HANDICAP IN THE MIDDLE AGES

For hundreds of years, communities in England dealt with mental illness and mental handicap as two separate issues. The mentally ill were burnt at the stake or drowned as witches; the mentally handicapped were given or assumed important positions in the community — as in court fool, court jester or village idiot. There were strong views that the birth of a handicapped child was a punishment for the sins of the parents. Folklore throughout the centuries makes reference to normal babies being stolen by the devil and changelings (handicapped babies) being left in their place. For the changeling, the care it received was of a very high standard. Families and communities believed that, if any harm came to the changeling, the devil would harm the normal child. Mothers of handicapped babies were at times branded as witches, and were accused of having intercourse with the devil, which resulted in the birth of a handicapped child. An interesting aspect of the early history of how communities came to terms with handicap is that each community was able to place the blame for the handicap on an outside force. Forces of evil were usually the major contributing factors. All these things suggest that somehow the community had to have a reason for why the handicapped baby had been born. By being able to place the blame somewhere, anywhere, this made the problem far easier to deal with and to come to terms with for parents and communities.

As with most injustices of life, having some sort of reason for why they happen or having some rational explanation doesn't change the injustice, but it does give something tangible on which to be able to reason it through. Kings and lords saw to it that mentally handicapped members of their community were treated with respect. They took responsibility for them and provided them with a higher standard of living than their common peers. Today we do not regard the mother of a handicapped baby as being in league with the devil — but we do look for somewhere to apportion the blame. If there is a reason for why something is as it is, then it is much easier for us to come to terms with that. Many mothers have told me that, following the birth of their handicapped child, they lived with the daily questions of something lacking in themselves that had caused the handicap. In the past, the Swiss were the only community that had a positive outlook towards handicap. They believed that having a handicapped child was a sign that God favoured their family. It was a gift from Heaven. The services that we offer our handicapped community today might be very different if all nations and cultures had adopted this way of thinking. But they didn't.

HISTORICAL BACKGROUND

The service that is operational today has been influenced by social, legal, medical, educational and political changes and policies over many years. It serves no purpose to accuse various governments of slowness and reluctance to implement changes that have been proposed. Neither is it productive to

criticise various departments for their shortsightedness and
ignorance for holding back necessary legislation to provide
the handicapped sector with better circumstances.

During my research for this book, I originally intended to
list various legislative documents — leaving the reader to
reach his or her own conclusions about what various societies
and cultures have done, or rather what they have not done.
The information collected very soon became lengthy and
extensive — far surpassing the requirements for a book such
as this. To do any justice to the part that legislative process
plays in the history of mental handicap, the subject needs to
be dealt with separately. The reader therefore is strongly
urged to undertake his or her own research — the results will
be both surprising and alarming.

For myself, the most obvious factors arising were the
following:

(i) Governments have instigated many educational changes
and policies for children — normal children. Handicapped
children are always last on priority lists. When their turn has
come round, there has been absolutely no parity of esteem
whatsoever.

(ii) Proposals that have been made are nearly always shelved
for many years — financial implications prevent implementa-
tion.

(iii) Pressure from voluntary organisations and agencies
ultimately bring about changes. Campaigners for better rights
and better standards of care 'battle' continually against all
odds to make changes occur and to bring the care of handicapped people into line with other caring professions. This
state of affairs has existed for over 150 years. In the 1980s
campaigners are still having to battle relentlessly, even harder
than they did in the last century. If the work of the voluntary agencies eased up even a little, then a backward slide
would commence — hard to believe in this day and age.
Would respective governments have made the changes that
have occurred without this pressure being brought to bear? It
is sad and shameful to think that they might not.

(iv) Terminology used to describe handicapped people has
been appalling. Thankfully, we have progressed beyond
'idiots', 'imbeciles' and 'feeble-minded'. 'Mental defective' is

seldom used today, but how often do we still hear 'retarded' and 'subnormal'? In 1978, when the Warnock Committee finalised its report, 'educationally subnormal' was changed to 'children with learning difficulties'. In 1982, the Mental Health (Amendment) Act changed 'subnormality' to 'mental impairment'.

For all the campaigning that has been undertaken, we have done very little to 'improve the image'. My own use of the word 'handicap' at times leaves me with an uncomfortable feeling. It is better than using 'imbecile', but it still feels wrong. My admission to this I trust will go towards future generations being able to forgive my use of the word, as we seemingly appear to be forgiving of those practitioners and legislators who went before us. In undertaking some further reading of the historical background, it is worth noting that legislation does not simply apply to one particular discipline. Health and Education Departments have both produced various documents that need to be read in conjunction with each other. Suggested references for further reading can be found in Appendix 4.

Looking at the Family

PREGNANCY

Pregnancy is an emotionally upsetting time for all expectant parents. It is a time for planning and for changes. The arrival of a new member into the family undoubtedly gives rise to role conflict for parents. The mother-to-be pursuing a career has to come to terms with drastic alterations in lifestyle; the father-to-be has to learn to cope with changes of attention. Whether the pregnancy is planned or not, the arrival of the baby will radically alter routines and relationships.

For many parents, there are very real fears that the baby may be handicapped. The advancements made in antenatal care and the extensive technological methods now being used on a much wider scale can provide reassurances that the pregnancy is going according to plan. If the foetus is suspect to handicap, parents have the option to terminate the pregnancy. For some parents, this option is the only one that they feel able to take. But for many, the decision to go ahead with the pregnancy, despite the possibilities of a handicapped child being born, is often the one that is chosen. The subject is a very emotive one; situation and circumstance vary so much from one family to another. Having provided the parents with the facts in an objective way, the professionals must provide the necessary support to enable the parents to come to terms with and work through their decision. Moral issues may be involved, but they should not interfere with the welfare of the parents. Unless we have been in the situation for ourselves, then we really cannot begin to know what it must be like. Many parents have told me that during pregnancy they discussed at length what they would do were their baby handicapped. Yet when the baby was born, they reacted in a totally different way. Our responsibilities are to provide the best possible care — not to overcomplicate the issue with our moral standards.

Case Study

Mr and Mrs Lucas had been married for three years and the relationship was under considerable strain. One of the contributing factors was that Mrs Lucas was very involved in her responsible and stimulating career and her husband felt rather threatened by this. The unplanned pregnancy was normal and in fact was thoroughly enjoyed by them both. They discussed what they would do were the baby born handicapped and decided that it would be something that they would never be able to come to terms with. The baby was born three weeks prematurely and was severely handicapped, both physically and mentally. The thought of leaving the baby in an institution was something that they could not bring themselves to do. The reality of the situation changed all their preconceived ideas and plans. They took their baby home. Their marriage is now healthy and happy. Mrs Lucas told me that, if Simon had been born a normal child, they would not be together today and their marriage would never have survived.

Some mothers have extensive tests during pregnancy to

eliminate the prospects of a handicapped baby being born, and then give birth to a handicapped child, although the indications were never there.

Case Study

At 28 Mrs Woods was pregnant with her first baby. The pregnancy was planned and, even though Mrs Woods was totally committed to her career, she had planned to have two children and return to work as soon as she was able. She was reassured throughout the pregnancy that everything was as it should be and her daughter was born with a normal delivery. Shortly after a vaccine the baby started to have fits, and it was soon established that in fact she was mentally and physically handicapped. Eventually coming to terms with the situation, some six years later, the Woods family decided to go ahead with their original plan to have two children. They had genetic counselling and Mrs Woods was assured from all the tests that her baby was going to be healthy. Their second child was also born handicapped.

Some mothers give birth to normal babies and only when certain milestones are not reached are they advised that their child is handicapped. Whatever the cause, be it known or unknown, the disruption to lifestyle that pregnancy incurs is nowhere near comparable to the disruption that follows. Whatever the circumstances that lead to the handicap, the parents are confronted with a situation for which they are totally unprepared.

The professionals involved in these early stages play a major part in the process. Although the advice that they offer may have a good ethical base, they will nevertheless be conveying some of their personal views in their suggestions and advice.

WHEN THE BABY IS BORN

The circumstances have changed. The excitement, the anxiety, the pain, the ritual of birth, have changed the circumstances and the people concerned.

Hypothesising before the birth is very different from having to deal immediately with the turn of events afterwards. But the situation must be dealt with straight away, and the pressure is on from the outset. Depending on hospital policy, one of two options are open to parents. It must be remembered that hospital policy can determine which line of events will subsequently follow.

One policy is to remove the baby from the mother immediately so that there is no physical contact between them. Counselling then follows and parents are advised about adoption or fostering procedures. Encouragement is given for the parents to leave the baby with the hospital, which will make all the necessary arrangements for the placement of the child.

Some hospitals encourage contact between baby and mother, working on the principle that, once contact has been made, then the mother will want to keep the baby. Up and down the country there are thousands of stories about what has happened to families during this time. Some mothers were given their babies and told to get on with it. Others were given the support and encouragement that they needed to be able to reach a rational and logical decision. Whatever the circumstances, whether there was an element of choice or not, the shock of a handicapped baby being born is something that will leave its mark on the parents for as long as they live.

Premature babies on life-support machines create problems for professionals and parents. Not being able to know for sure if the baby is in fact handicapped makes it incredibly difficult for those who have to make decisions about future care. The doctor may 'feel' that, should the baby survive, then it would survive with a handicap. The doctor is able to tell parents this but what he or she is unable to tell them is to what degree the child will be handicapped. For parents looking at their newborn baby, kept alive only by machinery, how can they possibly be expected to cope rationally with what the professionals are telling them?

The decision to switch the machine off is never made by just one person. With so many 'ifs', how can anyone be that certain that the baby will be handicapped? Does the decision-making process get easier if there are physical problems that can be seen? How much information are the parents given? Are they fully informed of the services that can be offered to them were they to choose to keep the baby? Given all that, how do parents learn to live with the decision that they eventually make?

Case Study

When Lawrence was born in 1961 profoundly handicapped, his parents were told that he would never walk, never talk — in fact, never do anything. They refused to believe this and embarked on an extensive programme of activity that would defy the professionals. Through sheer determination on their part, unaided by anyone, they started the long process of bringing Lawrence up at home. The battle was long and hard and brought heartache and despair, but progress was made. Lawrence is handicapped. But he does speak and is actively involved with so many activities; his life is very full and satisfying. He has won medals for athletic competitions, he swims, and he has a terrific sense of humour and a tremendous personality.

His parents were able to find the resources within themselves to bring all this about. His mother often recalls the words of the medical staff many years ago — and if they had listened to what was said then, Lawrence would not be alive today. Living with his handicap is far less painful than having to live with the knowledge that they could have consented to switch off the machinery all those years ago.

AFTER THE BABY IS BORN

How can we ever begin to understand the turmoil and conflict that occurs following the birth of a handicapped baby? — the soul searching; the disbelief; the thousands of answers to thousands of questions that are never forthcoming but desperately needed; the sense of failure and despair. Parents somehow have to reconcile the fact that through them a handicapped baby was born. Acknowledging their 'failure' and learning to live with it is overwhelming. The plans that were made have now to change.

As with all trauma in our lives, we seem to cope much better if we are able to apportion blame. If we can have some concrete reasons as to why something has happened, although it does not make it any less painful, it certainly helps us to deal with it more effectively.

Why us? What is the reason for this terrible burden being inflicted upon us? What can we have possibly done that deserves such a tragedy? In the quest for the answers, parents very often take the baby to private consultations to establish something tangible. Driven by desperation that there has been some terrible mistake — and someone somewhere has got to be able to provide the evidence of this — parents see consultant after consultant in the search for a cure and an answer. Although they may know in their hearts that there is no cure, the obsession to explore every eventuality drives them on. The process becomes almost ritualistic. Knowing that they are seeing a consultant the following week, they are able to use this to enable them to get through the next few days. The prospects for the future are bleak. The hope that the 'next person' will hold the magic cure provides the energy to carry on.

Eventually, though, there comes a time when the reality of the situation is all too apparent. The facts are hard and cruel. The baby is not going to improve — the prognosis is poor. It is up to the parents to find whatever it takes, from within themselves, to prepare them for the future — very often a future that they cannot see.

Case Study

In 1970 when Mrs Simpson was told that her baby was profoundly handicapped, she refused to believe it. The medical staff were sympathetic but could offer little in the way of positive and immediate help. Mrs Simpson snatched up her baby from the cot and ran out of the hospital screaming. She could not believe that nothing could be done.

With the help of her GP and Health Visitor, she started a very extensive physical programme with Rachel. She worked day and night and, by the time the baby was two years old, Mrs Simpson was exhausted physically and mentally. But she was able to see improvement, albeit slow, and it was this that drove her on. She was in a position to afford private sessions with a speech therapist and, as Rachel's communication skills improved, so did her mother's energy levels.

After any baby has been born, what is needed is lots of support. The parents of a handicapped child do not need to be continually reminded of how awful everything is. They know how awful it is. They know that there is no justice. They know that things will get harder. They need to know that their families and their friends still care about them. This cannot be done from a distance. The tendency is to stay away, afraid that something that may be said will only hurt the parents more.

Parents need to be loved and need to be valued. Their self-esteem has taken quite a battering. They need to feel the involvement of something normal — normal friendships, normal relationships, normal patterns. Well-meaning friends who stay away are depriving them of the very things that they need most — contact. The parents can so easily become isolated from the life that they had before the birth. This only reinforces the guilt and the despair even further.

Case Study

Mr Brown was repulsed by any form of handicap or deformity. He made hurtful statements and often joked about anyone whom he felt was not normal. When his daughter was born in 1951 severely mentally handicapped, his first reaction was to run away and pretend that it had not happened. He did not run away, though. He stayed and devoted many long years in an effort to provide a better world for her to live in. He didn't even question whether she would be more appropriately cared for within an institution. He felt that this was God's punishment for how he had behaved towards handicap in the years before his daughter was born. He lives with the daily belief that fate took steps to punish him.

Case Study

In 1957 Mrs Green gave birth to a girl, normal pregnancy and normal delivery. She was not her first baby. The medical staff informed her husband that they thought the baby was handicapped and it would be in the mother's best interests if she was not told. In interview she said, in retrospect, that she knew that there was something that wasn't quite right with their daughter, but she couldn't put her finger on what it was. When she asked her husband what he thought, he always evaded the issue, and reassured her that everything was as it should be. When the baby was six months old the truth came out. She was not only confronted with the fact that her daughter was handicapped, but discovered that her husband had known all along, and had kept it a secret from her. Because a professional had advised her husband, he thought it not to be his place to question it. He suffered so much during those six months, daily having to live with the lies he was telling his wife.

With the best intentions in the world, whoever advised this course of action precipitated a rift in their relationship that was never to heal.

Case Study

Mrs Blackstone desperately wanted to be a mother. When she met and eventually married her husband, she continually talked about having children. Mr Blackstone wasn't too keen on having a family straight away, but within a year of their marriage, in 1959, they were parents of a handicapped girl. Mr Blackstone blamed his wife. He could only rationalise the situation by saying that it was because she had rushed things and trapped him that the child was not normal. Faced with the prospect of having to spend the rest of his married life trapped with both wife and child, he decided that this was something he was never going to be able to come to terms with — ever. He left home when the baby was four months old.

Case Study

Pauline, a severely handicapped child, was two years old when her father left home in 1966. She had two brothers aged three and five, and an older sister who was six. Her father was unable to cope with the pressures and felt that it would be best for everyone if he left. He was beginning to show signs of taking his revenge out on the other children and actually left home before his emotions got the better of him.

THE FORMATIVE YEARS

Having a baby around the house, it automatically follows that the workload and the pressure are increased. In families where there are other children, mothers have often said that the workload involved in caring for the handicapped child, physically, is very much the same as the work for a normal child. The anxiety levels, however, are higher as the parents are more aware of adverse signs of something being wrong.

Many people would argue that, until the baby reaches its first birthday, there is very little difference between the handicapped child and the normal child, in terms of actual care. Parents resign themselves to the constant routine of feeding, changing, sleeping, crying. It is what is expected of *every* baby. For many profoundly handicapped children the pattern set in these early months remains the pattern that will stay for the rest of their lives.

The milestones that normal children reach are sometimes never reached with a handicapped child. When the baby is small, the parents are responsible for all its needs. The baby is totally dependent on its parents. Unable to communicate exactly what it wants, at any given time, the parents have to be aware of signals given out and be able to interpret them accordingly.

In a normal child this phase is soon over and, as speech develops and coordination powers are increased, the child is able, in part, to tell its parents just what is needed at that particular time. Special codes of communication are established between the parents and the child. Outsiders to the close family unit very often have to have a translation of

what the baby or child is trying to say. As the child eventually develops communication skills further, there is less
need for any translation as the child is able to communicate
quite independently of its parents.

For the child who has physical problems and is immobile,
or for the child who has not developed speech, dependence
on the parents is heightened. The parents take on the role of
anticipating and interpreting every possible sign. As the communication channels are only one-way, the parents have no
idea if their interpretations are correct or not.

ONE-WAY COMMUNICATION CHANNELS

As the handicapped child grows older, its physical and mental
abilities often remain static. The parents then find themselves
in the position of having to care for the baby intensely, not
just for a year or eighteen months but for as long as the child
will live. The physical demands placed on the parents become
greater as the child becomes older and heavier. The pressure
continues. The parents are spending the entire day coping
with the increasing problems of their child, until such time as
provision is made for the child to attend either nursery or
school.

It is always surprising just how adaptable people can be
when the situation demands it. If these same parents had
been asked before their baby was born if they thought they
were capable of putting in these long hours of this demanding
work for x number of years, then they would probably all
have said 'no'. But circumstances do change people, and,
before they knew where they were, they had established
arduous routines that became the pattern that was to stay for
many years to come. Of course, tied up with this physical
energy were psychological processes. Having their child
dependent on them for their every need created the feeling of
being totally indispensable.

With a normal child, asking someone to baby-sit for an
evening or a couple of hours is something that all parents can
do, without having to worry about anything specific. Should
the child awaken, then easy steps could be taken to give the
reassurance necessary for the child to go back to sleep. During

a child's waking hours, there are lots of games and distractions that can be employed to keep the child amused.

For a handicapped child, there will rarely be the opportunity for them to be in the hands of a baby-sitter. Parents, rightly or wrongly, feel that the problems associated with the child are too hazardous to leave in the hands of a baby-sitter — no matter how capable they may be. Added to this is the fact that the parents have, by now, accustomed themselves to the belief that they are the only people who can understand what it is that their child wants. By virtue of the fact that they are with the child for twenty-four hours a day, it naturally follows that other people could never be able to understand the situation as well as they can.

It becomes a vicious circle. The more time they spend with the child, the harder it becomes to leave them. On the occasions when they do leave the baby, they are continually worrying about what is happening in their absence. The anxiety caused destroys any enjoyment they may have had from the 'escape'. This, in turn, leads them to believe that it just isn't worth it. And so the pattern is set.

During the past twenty years there have been noticeable changes within the caring professions with regard to handicap, and many disciplines now include this section in training courses. But parents who were struggling to keep mind and body together as recently as the 1960s were very much left to their own devices. Without the support of outside agencies, they arrived at what was for them a working solution to their problems. Not having the luxury of a shoulder to cry on, and for some, being isolated from their own families and rejected by friends, they did the best they could in the circumstances.

This category of parent not only suffered the daily anguish of their child's problems but also had to come to terms with the isolation that was imposed upon them by various sections of the community. Baby clinics were staffed by people who were well used to dealing with normal babies but found it impossible to do anything constructive for the baby with a handicap. Surrounded by this type of environment, the parents very soon came to believe that maybe it would be better just to battle on on their own, rather than to 'bother' other agencies, who obviously had so much work to do with other children who were clearly more deserving. Feeling guilty about their child having the slightest problem, they tended to keep away from GP surgeries, actually believing that there was little that could be done to make the situation any easier. The family retained its cocoon-like status and, as the years progressed, their lives became more and more inward looking and introverted.

SOCIALLY

Throughout the many interviews that I have conducted with parents, there began to emerge quite clear patterns of how families coped with the isolation. Some parents picked up the threads of their social lives before the baby was born and ran their households in the nearest way to normal that they could get. They chose friends who could be normal with them — doing normal things in normal ways. By deliberately keeping away from the contact that they could have had with other handicapped families, they felt they were holding onto and maintaining a normal lifestyle. Other families lost all contact with their previous social circles. The arrival of a handicapped baby into the family threw them into contact with other handicapped families and this then became the social norm.

Inevitably there is a group who slot in between the two — keeping contact with handicapped and non-handicapped families. As needs vary, so social behaviour changes and adapts. The first group described are, in my opinion, in the minority, yet appear to be much happier and far more outgoing in their approach and attitudes to care. One mother told me that she had enough handicap in her life without spending her free time dwelling on it further. Her time away from her child was engineered to recharge her batteries — in stimulating conversation and the company of a social circle removed from handicap. To have spent her time with other parents of handicapped children would have depleted her energy reserves and contributed to the depressing prospects of what life had in store for her.

Good support mechanisms are necessary to be able to strike a happy balance between the two. But too much time spent with handicap narrows the vision, clouds issues and inhibits progress. Too much time away results in losing touch with what's going on. The practitioner must have a healthy outlook on the part they can play in bringing a compromise to parents and guardians.

WHAT HAPPENS AFTER I'M GONE?

In the majority of cases, the handicapped person will inevitably outlive the parents. In realistic terms this means that the practitioners will be responsible for providing care until the child or adult dies. Death and the repercussions of what may follow are two very important issues that parents are now starting to face. Trusts have been established and financial provision can be made. But many parents still believe that they will outlive their children and be in a position to care for them for ever. The most painful argument for trying to promote even the most minimal levels of independence is the fact that this is often not the case.

Many parents believe that time spent at home is best and refuse all suggestions of even short-term care for their child. Unsure about what happens in hostel or hospital, parents can be very defensive about relief admission. Some regard it as an indication that they are unable to cope. Others see no value in having a break. Their lives are so much centred around their handicapped child that they are unable to function as a couple if the child is not there. Others feel that they cannot manage financially with the benefits lost through admission. The list is endless. In the vast majority of cases, the intentions are good. The tragedies occur when there is an unforeseen incident. Parents then find themselves in a position of being unable to offer the care they are used to providing. Their own illness or admission to hospital is a good and frequent example.

With circumstances beyond their control, the child or adult is admitted to residential care in an emergency. The sudden change of environment causes stress and upset. The child unfamiliar with change in surroundings will often react in a very unfavourable way. This only reinforces the negative atttitudes that parents hold with regard to the institution. The unsettled behaviour is seen as being caused by the institution, whereas it is the emergency that has brought it about. For the child familiar with stays in a residential setting, such emergencies are taken in their stride — with stress levels greatly reduced. With a consistency in patterns of learning life skills, reinforced by all environments, any transition that may have to be made from home to institution will be far more manageable.

In non-handicapped households, children grow up and ultimately leave home. Using their skills they make lives of their own independent of their parents. Likewise, parents breathe sighs of relief as their time becomes more their own — to pursue interests and hobbies free of their children. Unable to allow opportunities for change for the handicapped child is not only limiting the experiences for that child but inevitably limiting the experiences for those parents.

Looking at the Child

BOUNDARIES

Our codes of living are based upon experiences we gain throughout our lives. Children copy their elders, experiment with their peers and explore on their own. Parental figures set the boundaries, and it is within those boundaries that the child learns. For the normal child, their questions are answered and there is opportunity to be creative and spontaneous. The handicapped child has a very different code.

ADULT-BASED CHILDHOOD

Without the use of speech, there can never be any answers to questions that are never asked. Without the daily contact of other children, there can never be the opportunity to play with peers. Many handicapped children spend their lives in the company of adults, with little time for contact with children of their own age. Although the play of an adult is important, it is not providing the stimulation and room for exploration that can only be attained from play with another child. If play is always adult-centred, then the adult is setting the boundaries and establishing the rules. The child is not in a position to decide on the terms of reference. If the child is immobile, this limits the situation even further. Not having the body control to move from one position to another restricts the child to a degree that we could never appreciate — unless we had experienced similar trauma ourselves.

PHYSICAL RESTRICTIONS

Trying to see the situation through the child's eyes is something that we must attempt to do. For the immobile child there is no choice about position. As carers, we sit people up when they want to lie down and lie them on their backs when they want to lie on their stomachs. We must imagine what we would feel like if we were placed in a prescribed position that we did not want to be in. Do we give enough thought to how the child feels when we decide on their position?

EXPLORATION AND CREATIVITY

The handicapped child has much clearer boundaries set for it than the normal child. The severely handicapped child is not allowed to do anything. For twenty-four hours of every day, their every action is being watched by someone. If they lift a hand to take something up, then a watchful adult inevitably removes the object from reach. There is a similar pattern for normal children. But eventually the normal child will be allowed to hold the object, or at least have some explanation as to why they cannot: 'It's breakable.' 'It's hot.' 'It's dangerous.' The handicapped child is not afforded the luxury of such explanation. The handicapped child experiences a continual removal of objects that need to be explored. The adults are preventing the child from exploring their creative elements. They are reinforcing negative aspects of exploration.

It can be compared to having an electric shock each time we reach for the biscuit tin. Given enough shocks we would soon get the message that reaching for the biscuit tin just wasn't worth the reaction. This is exactly what happens to the child. As the years go by, the pattern is perpetuated. The child eventually stops exploring, as it becomes much easier for them not to do anything. There is no point really. Every time they try to touch something, they are given a negative response. Much better not to touch, with the added bonus, of course, that this pleases parents and staff. Not being in the position to say 'no' makes life a lot easier. The handicapped child is only allowed to experiment with objects that are prescribed by the adults. Not for them the joys of playing in a muddy puddle or discovering that snow is cold and makes mittens wet.

For the normal child, Christmas and birthdays are times of the year when they are able to indulge in some of their whims and fancies. I remember when I was eight years old, I begged and pleaded with my father to make me a toy shop. I wanted to be a shop assistant when I grew up and thought it would be great fun to practise early. My best friend at the time asked Santa for a nurse's uniform. When the novelty had worn off, we both arrived at our individual conclusions. I thought it would be much better if my sister took over the shop, and I hated having to be Elizabeth's patient! Similarly, she soon got fed up with fetching and carrying for me as I lay on my sick bed. By the following February we had both changed our minds with regard to our respective future careers. The next Christmas similar patterns were repeated using different ideas. But at least we were given the opportunity to experiment with them.

This type of pattern is repeated throughout childhood. The normal child gathers information as a variety of things are tried and tested. Eventually a preference for certain activities will emerge — the artistic, the scientific, the mechanical, the musical, and so on. Parents seeing these developments will either encourage or discourage, depending on their own views. But the child will at least have the opportunities to experiment with their own particular interests. For the handicapped child, many of the normal experimental games are not available to them. If it is presumed that the child will never make a cup of tea, then it is unlikely that this child will find a toy kitchen in their Christmas stocking. The games that allow normal children to experiment with life skills before they are old enough to experience the real thing are often the games that the handicapped child will never come across.

The lower the expectations of the child, the lower the standard of experimental gaming. Safe games and safe activities create more security for the adults. In a sense the handicapped child becomes protected from the rough-and-tumble world that the normal child experiences. Hampered very often by physical handicaps, their world becomes very limited.

NOT GREAT EXPECTATIONS

For a normal child the 'system' invests time, expertise and money into providing an educational base. When the normal child leaves school, there are provisions for further educational input to continue. This is, by and large, a decision that is taken by the child or young adult. Obviously there are various outside factors that are operational, but a school-leaver does have the choice about what they are going to do. If they have decided that they want to stop educating themselves, then this is something that they are at liberty to decide. Their basic education has provided them with sufficient skills to be able to cope with the outside world and to take the first steps along the road to independence.

For the handicapped child, there are no hard-and-fast rules that can dictate the level the child will be at once school-leaving age is reached. It would be a marvellous thing if all children leaving special schools at nineteen were fully equipped with social and life skills and able to care for themselves independently in the community. Some come through the system better than others.

The profoundly handicapped child needs more than the years at school to be able to develop to their full potential. The learning process is one that continues for life. It is hard to imagine how it must feel to be on the receiving end of learning a skill that may take up to thirty years to acquire — if ever. Development can be slow and minimal — taking months and sometimes years for progress to be made. Is it any wonder that parents and staff at times give up on trying out new ideas? Having to wait years for a response makes it difficult to believe that what is being done is being done in the right way. If a parent is teaching their child to fasten shoe laces or hold a spoon, and if twenty minutes each day is devoted to nothing but teaching these skills, with little results, can we be surprised that tempers are frayed? For the child, they not only have to come to terms with the frustration of not being able to do it — or not wanting to do it — but they also have to cope with the irritation of the person who is teaching them. Rather than struggle on for years, with anxiety levels raised by both parties, isn't it much easier just to let the adult do it? The task in hand is completed in faster time, anxiety levels are kept to a minimum and time is saved. Does it really serve any purpose to wait for thirty or forty years for the child to be this independent? After all, we're only talking about fastening shoe laces and holding spoons.

THE PETER PAN SYNDROME

The child who stays a child; the child who grows to adulthood without the recognition of ever getting there; the thirty year old who presents as a four year old — how difficult it is to have this strange combination. For the parent, to have to dress their son or daughter in adult clothes and yet see the child. For the child to look like an adult, yet be unable to function as one. The dependence as a baby continues well into adult life. For the carer, locked within the role that is forced upon them because of the dependence of the situation, there is no respite.

The child, though ageing, will rarely gain independence — so the roles for both parties will remain static. But as the roles remain static, then so does the progress. As milestones are not reached, the child is surrounded by reinforcement of their childhood. Pleased by the slightest progress made, parents and staff tend to get stuck with the 'childhood'. Arriving at what seems to be a workable situation, with energy levels draining, the carers accept the Peter Pan syndrome. Things are manageable, people are coping and the 'child' is happy. This is where the conflict arises — when we are faced with breaking habits of a lifetime.

To be realistic, what we have to remember is that we can readily justify all our actions. We know that it is easier if we

can do it; we know that it is quicker if we do it; we know
that it is less anxiety-provoking if we do it. Does the child
know this? How do they feel? Do they like us doing everything for them? If roles were reversed, would we? Would we
be content with Peter Pan status all our lives?

Looking at the Staff

WHO CARES?

Working with profoundly handicapped people is a specialist
field demanding specialist skills. For many disciplines involved in mental handicap, this is an area that either appeals or
does not. There are no shades of grey. I have met very few
people who have appeared to be indifferent to this type of
work. Most people know instinctively if they are going to be
able to cope with it or not. As with most professions, the
interest and enthusiasm for the work is the directing force at
play.

But working with a severely handicapped group places
physical demands on staff. My own feelings are that age, in
most cases, is irrelevant. The priority issues lie in the attitudes
towards the work. The ability to create a stimulating environment, and be able to monitor and maintain it, should be the
criterion for deciding who will care. The multidisciplinary
approach will always yield the best results — each discipline
offering the expertise that is most appropriate to each
individual. Energy levels of staff have to run high to maintain good standards of practice — to record, monitor and
chart progress made and unmade, and always to have a clear
sense of direction. The ability to liaise with parents, guardians
and other disciplines involved is vital. The realities command
determination and hard work, with expectations of some, but
minimal and slow, progress. To function in an area with
severely handicapped children or adults therefore demands
certain attributes from the staff.

It is crucial to the well-being of all handicapped people in
any care setting that staffing placements are appropriate. I
have often heard it said that no extra staff at all would be

better than someone being placed who does not want to be there. Other staff members are able to comment on colleague's placements. But the handicapped child has little if any opportunity for being able to voice their opinions.

THE ISOLATION OF SPECIAL CARE UNITS

For many Adult Training Centres, hospitals and special schools, the Special Care Departments, although part of the overall establishment, are geographically set apart from the main building. The reasoning behind this is, in part, logical. The day-to-day comings and goings are contained in one area. The work is usually more successful without added interruptions that would occur in the main building. Meal times are more containable — the list is endless.

The damaging effect of this system though is isolation. Profoundly handicapped people are isolated from higher-ability people. Staff are isolated from their colleagues — resulting in an overall feeling of being cut off. Breakdown of communication can be a common occurrence if units are physically isolated. Unless communication channels are actively encouraged to be a two-way process, then misunderstandings between unit and main building will inevitably occur. Good support systems for staff in Special Care Units are vital. But this can be a problem when units function in isolation.

Those who are continually in a low-ability setting, although they may feel secure, will have little opportunity to copy more 'normal' behavioural traits. Not having the time to mix with higher-ability groups can very often hinder their progress rather than enhance it. Staff, too, can become trapped in the severity of the handicap, deprived also of higher-ability functioning — which drains resources. A happy medium must be sought for all parties. Time out, no matter how minimal, ought to be available for both parties at regular intervals. Inviting other staff and groups into the unit can also be a positive way of changing the isolation. I am not advocating that the doors should be flung wide for open house, but selective activities could be arranged to accommodate people from other areas. This allows others to see what is going on and stimulates interest, albeit on a sessional basis.

THE PROFESSIONALS

The most important criteria for anyone, professional or otherwise, to be employed to work in a Special Care Unit must be that they *want* to work there. I believe that there is a place for the untrained worker, but I will deal with this issue later on. 'Professional' immediately conjures up for me thoughts of 'discipline' and 'training'. As with many fields of work, the discipline of training creates an inner discipline within the practitioner. Although each particular discipline follows a prescribed training pattern, there are areas that overlap across the professions.

Within a Special Care Unit there can never be enough professionals. Psychologists, instructors, nurses, medics, occupational therapists, physiotherapists, speech therapists, social workers, teachers — all have very important roles to play. Add to this list music therapists, dramatherapists, art therapists, dance therapists, any therapist, and the overall spread of expertise provides enormous resources that can be drawn upon.

It must be remembered that no one discipline will have within its own training structure long periods of time devoted specifically to the profoundly handicapped child or adult. The subject area may have been covered at some point during training along with other aspects of care for the handicapped, but the majority of training courses do not facilitate full-time study of this sector. It is usually during this period that the training professional gains insight into the area — formulating ideas as to whether this will be a field in which they can eventually work, or not. Coming into the Special Care Unit, therefore, can initially create problems in that the professional is aware of what he or she can do in lots of other sectors (more clearly defined areas) but has no firm ideas as to how his or her particular expertise can be applied to this specific group. The most difficult aspect to come to terms with is how the theory and previous practice of the discipline can be adapted to the Special Care setting.

MODELS

Depending on the funding of the Special Care Unit, the NHS,

Education Department, Social Services Department, whatever, will dictate the initial model employed for the unit as a whole. Someone has to be in overall charge of the management of the unit, and this generally provides the base for the strategies employed. An educational-based unit in a special school will undoubtedly be run along educational lines — adopting educational policies and principles. A hospital-based unit will undoubtedly be organised along the lines of medical model strategies.

It is very important that, whatever discipline is in the driving seat for the unit, the particular discipline is not the only one that has any say in what goes on. Good qualities of leadership and management are, of course, very important but there needs to be so much more. The leader or director has to recognise the qualities in other professions that are necessary to provide a comprehensive programme. We might all like to think that our respective professions are adequate enough to provide the service required, but in reality this is far from true. This is where the multidisciplinary team really comes into play. Each discipline must feel able to contribute to the running of the unit. Having the opportunity to make suggestions is not enough. Time must be made available to try the suggestions out. Having a multidisciplinary team approach in operation will never be the answer to everyone's problems. There needs to be a 'togetherness' in attitude towards care. Each person must be seen to be a complete person, with very special and individual needs. Sometimes we have to isolate aspects of behaviour in an effort to treat — but this should never be done in isolation of the person as a whole. The separate disciplines must have clear ideas as to what it is that they can offer the care setting and the ability to be able to use the resources accordingly and appropriately.

It is crucial to the well-being of handicapped people that decisions are made with regard to treatment programmes and activities are made in consultation with all the parties concerned, and I include parents and guardians in this decision-making process. Unless everyone involved is fully aware of what the aims and objectives are, then what very often happens is that each worker ends up following a path of out-of-context activity that bears no relation to work being done in other areas.

TRAINING

Having completed some form of professional training must never lead us to assume that we now know it all. We know what *we* know, but we do not know what other disciplines know. As interest grows in this field of work, there are constant advertisements in established therapy and nursing press for seminars, workshops, short courses and conferences. A valuable aspect of attending training sessions is that it brings staff into contact with others working in the field. It is a well known fact that the interesting discussions that go on during tea breaks are very often far more stimulating than the seminars themselves! Sometimes just being able to make contact with others can be the most therapeutic part of training. Finding out that there are other people struggling with similar problems can be comforting and consoling, and can take away some of the isolation.

IN-SERVICE TRAINING

Training costs time and money — factors that are not always easily available. This does not mean that training should be out of reach. Is there a particular subject that interests you greatly? Could you talk about it for half an hour? Could you do this in a lunch break? Do you work alongside someone who seems to have a particular interest or skill? Is there a colleague who you would like to spend more than a snatched tea break with? Can they tell you more about what it is they are doing? Would they be prepared to do this at lunch time?

There you are — instant in-service training!

Being a professional not only makes us responsible for those people in our care, it should also make us responsible for training others. Just because we have spent years working hard for a qualification doesn't mean that we have to keep it all to ourselves! If every discipline opened up a little bit more and spread their word, then we would all become more enlightened, and we all stand to gain.

WITHOUT TRAINING

I believe that there is a valuable role for the untrained worker
to play in any Special Care Unit. Again, the criterion for
employment must be that they are motivated to work there.
There are many part-time posts for untrained staff. Working
for half a day, or twenty hours each week, or whatever,
provides a very secure framework for people who want to
work in the field but are unable to take up a full-time position. The untrained eye is a marvellous thing. Not having the
prejudices of training allows a naivety in approach that is
often not experienced by trained staff.

I recall my time working in the community with a nursing
assistant who taught me everything there was to know. Her
life experiences had given her a much sounder grounding for
the work involved than my limited professional experience
had. It was she who opened my eyes to be able to see the
complete person. She was the one who could see each patient
in a natural way — I was too lost looking for labels.

On the whole question of staffing, what is important is
that the team work together in a happy and cohesive way.
Having a mix of the young and the old, the trained and the
untrained, can only be providing a greater pool of resources
upon which can be drawn those most appropriate.

TIME OUT

Time is at a premium. There are never enough hours in the
day to do all the things we need to do, let alone start thinking about doing something for ourselves. But this is an area to
which we must give very careful consideration. To be able to
work together as a team we must create opportunities to discuss aspects of care together. It is nearly always impossible to
get everyone involved together at the same time — but efforts
must be made for this to happen.

The discipline that we use in our work must spill over for
use for ourselves. Time must be made available for us to be
able to talk about our worries and concerns. If we bottle
things up, then who are the ones to suffer? They are the very
people we are trying to help. Having a meeting every month

is tedious and time-consuming. Issues that were important three weeks ago are not important now. Finding time each week to discuss problems enables them to be dealt with as they arise and before they are allowed to get out of hand. We would not allow handicapped people's problems to go unresolved indefinitely — so why make the distinction with ourselves?

WHO CARES ABOUT THE PEOPLE WHO CARE?

Working with profound handicap demands from us a realistic and practical approach. We need to be constantly aware of the boundaries that we are setting and making sure that our targets are within reach. We need to be ever aware of our own boundaries and limitations, as without these then our work becomes unnecessarily difficult.

In organising programmes, although the tendency is to centre the activities around the handicapped person with some consideration to staffing levels and resources, we make no provision for our own needs. If a handicapped child or adult is in our care for six hours of the day, then we feel we ought to be doing something for every minute of these six hours. I am suggesting that within this timespan we ought to be looking at taking some of this time for ourselves. It is not at all realistic to think that constantly being with a person is going to be in their best interests — or, in fact, in ours. This area of work demands an awful lot from staff, and by not taking time out we are preventing a clear overall view from emerging. Allocating some time of the day, or at the end of the shift, or before the child or adult goes home, enables the staff the opportunity to share feelings and ideas. Being able to share is very supportive.

The work at times is emotional and, without the facility for being able to discuss problems that arise, we often end up taking these feelings home with us. Without any opportunity for dealing with them, the feelings will become destructive, interfering with the work and attitudes of the very person who needs to keep mind and soul together. This is vital in order to provide an environment that will be conducive to the needs of those for whom we are caring. For those not used to taking time out, the very suggestion of doing so may conjure up immediate impossibilities of why it cannot happen. Time is the usual excuse. But given time to think about it there are literally hundreds of other excuses that can be used.

To be honest about it, the real issues are to do with the attitudes of the staff, and much less to do with the practicalities of the Unit. By somehow creating the opportunity to talk about one's work leads people to think that it will be an open forum for criticism about their work. The negative aspects always seem to be apparent. The reverse is the case. Finding the time to discuss your work and feelings is an acknowledgement of your value and your worth. It is the recognition of hearing what you have to say — what you feel — the very basis for working in this field. It facilitates the opportunity for colleagues to offer support and to share similar problems. Of course, there is an element of risk involved. It is unrealistic to believe that everyone who works with you will feel the same way. But it can be an invaluable forum for discussion, which enables all parties concerned in the care setting to see the picture from all angles.

It must be remembered that this field of work does not always provide instant feedback on work done. Very often there are no signals that what is being done is necessarily the right thing to do — or the right way to do it. The work is isolatory. Is it reasonable to ask all staff to keep everything to themselves? By doing this and not encouraging discussion, we are perpetuating isolation. How can we ever start to gather new experiences and new ideas if we do not share what we already have? How the time is found and in fact how it is utilised cannot be given on prescription. Each Unit, each school and hospital, is governed by their own individual systems. There is no right way of setting about this task. What I am trying to convey is the importance of finding the time.

If we are harbouring areas of conflict within ourselves, then this is only going to be transferred to those in our care. Finding a forum for dealing with our needs and, in a sense, our own handicaps, can only enhance and improve the way in which we work. The capacity for thinking up new ideas is not a process that will last for ever. We need to be stimulated and, in the therapeutic sense, we need to be fed. We can have all of this from each other. Finding ten minutes in a day is not asking for the impossible. We owe it to ourselves to have the discipline to take this time. We will never be able to put any value on our work if we are so narrow minded that we cannot value ourselves.

SUPERVISION

Student nurses, student therapists, student teachers, all students, have within their own peer groups the opportunities for counselling to take place, the opportunity to share experiences and be able to talk about their work and how they feel about various aspects of it. But this very valuable sharing experience, which abounds throughout training, in some cases disappears completely soon after qualification. It must be said, however, that this is not true of all disciplines. Working within the therapeutic model, the very essence of a therapist's work is based upon the reflection of what they are actually doing with the client group, with insight and aware-ness of their own feelings, to give better clarity and sense of direction in further planning. Through supervision, which is very much a reflective process of group work spoken to another party, any resolve that needs to be found, or loss of direction that needs to be relocated, or greater understanding of process that needs to be arrived at, can be reached in most cases by merely hearing what is being spoken out loud. The description of group or individual work, once verbalised, can be explored fully with another party. It is within this area of exploration that answers can be found. Without the explora-tion, questions remain unanswered, or, worse still, are never even considered worth asking.

Everyone working within the field of profound handicap needs support. We constantly need to know that what we are doing is right. Not only do we need this reassurance, but we also need to know when we are making mistakes. By allowing an opening for views and opinions to be shared, we can pro-vide our own counselling. Sharing a problem, and then discovering that someone else has the same problem, provides a very good base for looking at ways of finding a solution. Keeping it all to ourselves, the feelings, and the emotions, does far more harm than good.

As mentioned earlier, talking about the fears and worries of the work is not inviting open criticism about that work. Supervision is supportive and constructively caring. Yes, there are times when what might be said is painful, but better that it can be said early on, rather than not being said at all and some catastrophic incident following. Irrespective of the status of the discipline, there ought to be positive and constructive channels for supervision/counselling/support in operation for all.

On a personal note, I have always found it useful to have my own supervision from a discipline other than my own. This has afforded me the added bonus of being able to see and then resolve a problem through the eyes of a different professional model. But the main point of including supervision in this chapter is to stress just how important it is.

Profound handicap, by its very nature, takes very slow steps along the progress scale. For some children and adults, processes take years to achieve. Although everyone works very hard throughout these years to reach goals and set new objectives, because the length of time can be so great the original objectives frequently get easily lost. If progress is not being made, in any area, despite all the effort and hard work, then families and practitioners lose heart. This is all very understandable and nobody would argue with this point. But when we do give up and stop trying, what happens then to the person in our care?

With good counselling, good support systems and good supervision, this process need never come about. But if it does, then circumstances will never be as traumatic as those where counselling is not available. Profound handicap needs investment to keep heads above water. We know how difficult it can be at the best of times. Even on a good day, things can be pretty terrible. But we have a responsibility to make changes and improvements and always to be moving in the right direction — forwards. So what better way to move forwards? By supporting everyone involved in the caring process, in effect we will be supporting and improving the quality of life for profoundly handicapped children and adults in our care.

Charity beings at home. If we can't look after each other then can we seriously expect anyone else to?

2 Fighting Handicap: Looking More Closely at Some of the Problems

Transference

The realities of profound handicap are obvious — the difficulties of dressing, feeding, lifting, changing and so on. But beyond the physical complications lie a group of psychological problems and processes that often get lost or are simply forgotten. My intention here is to remind the reader of some of the problems of transference — briefly explained as a process whereby emotional and physical feelings are transferred from one person to another. Having a greater awareness of them will not take the handicap away. Insight will not make aphasics talk, it will not improve muscle tone and it most certainly will not repair damage that has already been done. But what it may do is provide us with a greater understanding of those we are working with — their families and of course ourselves. By blocking out the possibilities, either consciously or subconsciously, we are in effect fighting against the feelings and emotions. This only serves to complicate issues even further. By at least being open-minded enough in our approach to recognise that transference may be happening, we can leave ourselves with fewer obstacles to inhibit progress.

Case Study

Robin lived in a hostel for mentally handicapped adults. He was able to care for himself with little help from the staff. He formed a very close attachment to his social worker and a part-time therapist who visited the Centre each week. During an art therapy session, Robin painted what closely resembled two smashed cars. He explained that as social worker and therapist were talking about leaving the area, he thought that if they could crash their cars into each other and break their legs, then they would be unable to go anywhere. Robin was very angry with both of them but was unable to tell them just how angry he felt. He cared not that if they were in hospital he still would not be able to see them — he simply wanted to punish them. He wanted to transfer some of his hurt to them. He giggled uncontrollably at the thought of all this coming true. The only way he could cope with the situation was to derive some pleasure from their possible pain.

BEING HELPLESS

The overwhelming hopelessness of handicap can be a very powerful force: the adult who has to be lifted as one would lift a baby; the adult who cannot communicate or move; the adult who is totally dependent; the adult with a history of 'not responding to stimuli'. To be confronted with such profound handicap and be expected to 'do something' can be very daunting. The person is so helpless, and first impressions often are that there is little that can be done. These feelings of helplessness take over the situation, and the more profound the handicap, the greater the power. It is this power that renders the practitioner helpless. The aphasia, the spasticity, the contortion of limbs, the repulsion — all are displays of obvious helplessness that reinforce the despair and almost defy people to do something.

Unfortunately, the strength of the power often results in nothing being done and the unresponsive existence becomes the established pattern and way of life. This may sound hard, almost cruel, but it is very real. The process occurs with such frequency and I personally have experienced it many times. Being helpless is a strange feeling. Colluding with it only highlights the inadequacy further. My discomfort is always related to my impotence, not that of my client. But the rationale is easy. Presented with a hopeless, helpless case, where all previous attempts to do something have proved futile, if nothing is expected to be done then where is the failing in doing nothing? Can anyone be blamed for not doing anything?

Case Study

Geoffrey was twenty years old when he was transferred to the Unit. His attendance at school had been poor — colds, chest infections and influenza being the most common complaints. He was very profoundly handicapped, physically and mentally. His school records were forwarded to the Unit prior to his admission. Various reports had been written by teachers, educational psychologists and medical staff. There were two predominating themes in the file. Poor attendance due to ill-health had made consistency of work difficult. Total lack of response to any stimuli had prevailed throughout his time at school.

The picture that had been painted was a depressive one. Negative reports had, in effect, fed more negative reports. It was as if everyone involved had come to terms with the fact that nothing could be done for Geoffrey. His handicap was so severe that changes were impossible. This feeling came with him to the Unit. Nobody tried to pretend that things were other than they were. The prognosis was very poor. The major issue was whether the Special Care Unit could accommodate him, thereby giving the parents a break. Inevitably the question of staffing levels and current pressures were discussed — almost as if this was part of the rationale of not being able to offer very much more to this young adult and his family. The admission procedures were finalised.

Geoffrey was lifted out of his wheelchair each morning and laid on a blanket on floor mats. All members of staff spoke to him and he was encouraged to look at mobiles and 'play' with various toys. Physical contact was made at changing times, feeding times, bath times and so on. But the rest of the time Geoffrey was fairly isolated. It was impossible to include him in any group activities — the demands made by others in the group prevented the allocation of one member of staff being with him all the time.

When I was asked to 'do something with him', my immediate reaction was one of sheer horror. His hips were not to be load-bearing. This prevented any work being done from the waist down. He was difficult to lift and hold. Without speech or sound it was impossible to establish if any activity was pleasurable or painful. The involuntary movements of the arms made it difficult to move them in any way. He was very fragile, and had not been 'moved' in any real sense of the term for nearly seventeen years. I could not justify not doing anything with him, although I had no idea where I could start or what I could do. As I approached him and told him who I was, I was filled with terror.

As I lifted him into my arms, I could feel his heart racing. His pulse rate was 160. At the time it was as if I was clutching at straws, but this was a response. I held him in different ways and checked his pulse rate at five-minute intervals. After twenty minutes it had settled down to 120. This was still high — and not provoked by active movement, any effort physically made was my own.

My interest at this stage was purely reflective of having some sort of response. I had not really given much thought to doing anything specific. The restrictions placed upon me were terrific — but having something to work on, albeit raised pulse rates, was at least a start. Taking this as a base on which to work, we then started to monitor his pulse rates at different times during the day, during different activities. By the third week there was a noticeable difference. At the outset of a session with Geoffrey his pulse rate was 120, but this lowered to 90 and 80 after a period of about ten minutes. The anxiety caused by the new environment and the new faces could have been the contributing factor to the raised pulse rates.

Being picked up could also have been seen as being distressing to him. All the interpretations we discussed, of course, were only a hypothesis — Geoffrey was unable to tell us, or indicate, what the causes could have been. What was happening was that Geoffrey had somehow transferred his helplessness to me. I was very aware of how inadequate and impotent I was when working with him. In a sense, the helplessness and hopelessness of the situation was mine, not his.

This came as quite a shock. It is not easy to admit one's failings and inadequacies. Making statements that prove defeat is certainly not something that is encouraged. Parents and staff work along the lines of doing their best. To admit to not being able to do anything can be seen as 'giving up'. This is impossible to rationalise. There is no justification in 'giving up'. With Geoffrey, as with many Special Care people, there is no way to go but up. Things cannot really get much worse.

The next session I spent with him, I started off by telling him that he had won. I was absolutely at my wits end as to what to do. I was helpless. I had told the other members of staff and now I had told him. He turned his head round to face me, and tapping my arm, he smiled. It was almost as if he had been willing me to say it. The relief on my part was quite overwhelming. It was like setting down a heavy burden. I had only wished that I had been able to come to terms with my helplessness sooner. Simply acknowledging that it was there, cleared the way for things to be done. The hurdle had been overcome and, in a way, this had lowered the barriers on both sides and removed some of the distance between us.

How can anything be taught if the teacher is helpless? It is like trying to ride a bike without any wheels. It is not a failing on the part of staff to admit freely to these feelings. Keeping it inside only feeds the situation. It has to be admitted to colleagues — and most importantly, to the person concerned. The worst thing that can happen is nothing, but at the best it may produce a smile.

FEAR

Very closely linked to helplessness is fear. When working with profoundly handicapped people who are totally uncommunicative, there is no way of knowing if what is being done is right. When the only facial movements are dribbling, for those who are completely immobile, then how on earth can they ever tell the practitioner if something is wrong?

Fear of hurting, fear of causing distress, fear of speaking too quickly, fear of uncomfortable posture are all part of the transference problem. It must be a terrifying experience to be approached by a complete stranger in a strange setting. Pulse rates increase, agitation occurs and staff in turn then become hesitant and nervous. Because the situation is very unsafe, unsure of what is going to happen next, not knowing who these strange people are, anxiety levels inevitably will rise. Staff quickly pick up this anxiety, which in turn feeds their own. Before anyone has any time even to think about what is happening, these two factors combined render both parties fearful. The transference of anxiety quickly becomes a very active two-way process, which prevents any work from being done at all.

The ability to acknowledge what is happening will make the practitioner more relaxed and more aware of what is going on. If the anxiety levels of the practitioner can be reduced, then it will automatically follow that the anxiety levels of others will decrease also. As both parties start to relax then the contact becomes much safer. Safety and security will drive the fear away. Holding on to the fear will only reinforce it.

Can't Stop Now

THE BATTLING SYNDROME

I am sure that anyone involved in the field of handicap has witnessed the 'battling syndrome' at some time or another. It is more apparent in families of handicapped children born before the 1970s, although it is nearly always seen at some stage with all families and staff groups.

Changes in trends have enlightened many disciplines, resulting in an impressive comprehensive service being offered to parents of handicapped children. From birth, relevant and appropriate agencies become involved and support is given to parents to enable them to cope with their child at home. All this is as it should be. Opportunity play groups have been established, where handicapped children can play with normal children, and are given every encouragement to keep up to the same pace. From a very early age the handicapped child is in a stimulating environment, for a couple of mornings each week, allowing the parents some time off. Regular assessment is carried out in the early years to ensure that school placement is appropriate, and according to the child's needs and functioning ability at the time.

This is what is happening now but it was not like this years ago. Parents were told not to take the handicapped babies to clinics for weighing. 'We don't weigh that sort of baby here' was the frequent response from the professionals. One mother told me that, whenever she took her handicapped baby to the clinic, she was told that they 'didn't bother with that type of child'. Then, it seemed as if very few people, professional or otherwise, bothered at all. For those parents, the battle seemed inevitable. Specialists were few and far between, and although lots of disciplines knew a little, very few seemed to know it all.

Long-stay mental handicap hospitals were, of course, coping adequately with their situation, before the pioneers of community care became instrumental in widening horizons. But for families deciding on a life in the community for their handicapped child, the prospects were very bleak. Appalling lack of provision and resources drove many parents into action. Determined to do something, anything, working groups were established, associations were formed and money was raised. Pressure was brought to bear, both locally and nationally, and facilities were improved and Training Centres were built.

The movement into the community was a continual battle — for better services, better staffing levels, better equipment, better benefits — but once these were established, they did not halt the battling syndrome. All forms to be filled in were like declarations of war. Claims for one particular thing very often stopped another. Parents wanted to continue to be involved with their child's care — still striving for better things and not content in the main to sit back and become complacent. This pattern, once established, was difficult to break. Fighting for over twenty years for something better was not suddenly going to come to an end. Many parents became labelled: 'Pushy mother', 'Interfering father', and so on. For many the labels they acquired were merely reflections of their handicapped lifestyles thus far. Needless to say that for the complacent parents, no labels were attached. Having reaped some fruits of their labours, the 'pushy brigade' continued to battle and still do. Fund raising for new premises and equipment, political pressure for reform, are ongoing situations. Although one has to take each situation in context, it is understandable that some parents come across as being bitter and resentful. In most cases they have every right to be. Bringing up a handicapped child is not easy, and for the vast majority of parents this was a task that was undertaken and completed on their own, without any support systems operational.

To bring about any change in these long-standing feelings and attitudes is a difficult task. Not used to the idea of having a Social Worker, when confronted with one for the first time, usual comments are: 'I needed you years ago. I don't need you now.' With the best intentions in the world, opinions like this cannot be changed overnight. On the practical side, many of the issues have been resolved without the help of the outside agencies. What is missing from the picture is an established pattern of support throughout the early years. As the years go by, the urge and drive to battle may still be there, but the energy necessary to continue becomes somewhat dissipated.

CAMPAIGNING OR COMPLAINING?

As the child gets older, there are less pressing and urgent things to battle for. The child has been guaranteed day care for an indefinite period of time and the energy previously spent in campaigning, at this stage, very often goes into complaining. Complaints vary from activities, meals, monetary awards, accidents, loss of clothing and so on. In effect the battle is continued. Although the parent recognises the finality of the situation, they do not always necessarily come to terms with it. To trust someone else to care for their child, for many, does not come easily. No one can possibly look after their child as effectively as they can do at home — so they are very receptive to any small thing that may be wrong, and in most cases complain.

Parents need lots of attention for themselves — and complaints are very much a reflection of this need. There have been few people who have acknowledged their hard work over the years, and nobody has told them just how good a job they have done. All the hard work has not taken away the handicap or even relieved it — it is still there. The progress has been minimal and in some cases non-existent. A lifetime has been devoted to the child — to the exclusion of everything else, not least of which their own needs. At some point their own need for attention must surface. The child has taken everything they have had to give, and more. Giving so much can, and must, result in craving attention for themselves alone. One of the ways this manifests itself is in writing letters of complaint. The replies to these letters are an acknowledgement of attention. Clever letter writers will read the signs and ensure that attention, the *right* attention, is given.

Ideally, creating an environment whereby complaints are never necessary would suit all parties, but this is unrealistic. In agreeing to day care provision, the parent is isolating himself. If parents can be made to feel part of the progress and work that is going on through the day, although not physically present, then this opening up of communication channels can go a long way towards lowering anxiety levels. Any misunderstandings that may occur, and they do, can be more easily resolved if staff are accessible to parents, so that both parties are aware of the other's situation. Parents of severely handicapped children are concerned that there is no one who can speak for the child. Good relationships must exist between staff and parents, and everything necessary must be done to provide parents with the attention they need.

What Problems?

It is impossible to draw up a complete and comprehensive list of problems relating to profound handicap. As the topic is so complex and vast, I have tried to select a cross section of issues — the reader must pardon the omissions.

Behavioural disturbances create turmoil and upset — for everyone. There is always a tendency on the part of parents and practitioners to want continually to 'tidy things up' and keep things running on a very even keel. I am certainly not advocating that we all go out of our way to rock boats. But I do find it irritating when everything on the surface is analysed in detail — without going beyond the handicap to get to the real root of the problem. To interpret behaviour we must first of all understand it. In this section I am not setting out to provide an authoritative statement about some of these problems — merely giving them an airing.

TRUST

Trusting is a risky business. We tend to select carefully those people we confide in. There is power in trust and it is an aspect of our lives that we all take quite seriously. When confidences are broken, there is a feeling of hurt. When people we thought we could rely on let us down, we feel upset. Our defences guide us when we share a confidence. We are on our guard to keep safe secrets and persons entrusted to us. For the profoundly handicapped child or adult, there is very little choice in being able to exercise these normal selective processes. They may feel unsafe in certain surroundings and situations, but are unable to communicate verbally these feelings, and so at times have to live with the anxiety that this causes. For a normal child there are unlimited methods of expression that can be called upon to indicate distress. If an adult in play picks them up and this causes fear because the child feels unsafe, then they can soon communicate this both physically and verbally. For the handicapped child, being picked up can be a very stressful situation. Without the ability to communicate, this can aggravate stress levels further. We can allow stressful things to happen to us when we want

them to, and yet have a built-in mechanism to stop them happening if we wish. We must be careful when working with handicapped people that we are always aware of situations that may be stressful to them. Because we are the professionals, this does not inevitably mean that we are trustworthy people. We have to allow time for the person to find out that we can be trusted We have to be seen as being safe people. It is not enough to tell someone this — we have to demonstrate it by our actions at all times.

'Handle With Care', 'Fragile', 'Do Not Bend', ... For many handicapped people, having these labels is something that they have always had. Their physical states almost shout these things out at us. Contorted limbs and unnatural postures immediately start ringing warning bells to exercise caution when moving and lifting. What very often happens is that because we are so aware of these labels we tend to hesitate before lifting and, unsure of what we are doing, hold people in an unsafe way. Our anxiety levels are instantly raised, and this is easily transferred. Before very long there is a stressful situation for both parties.

Of course, we have to be very careful when lifting and moving profoundly handicapped people, and I am not at all suggesting that handling should be rough. However, firmness of hold is far more reassuring than a light touch. If held in a secure manner this will give confidence, both to the child or adult and to the worker. Once people feel that the lifting is safe, then they will not be resistant to this movement. For us to be trusted we have to come up with the goods. Being able to recognise distress signals and interpret needs and act accordingly will help to improve the relationship and create a safer environment. Unfortunately, lots of the signals are very obscure. Keen observation powers are needed all the time.

PARENTAL TRUST

Parents sometimes find themselves in the position of having to trust people and situations of whom and of which they are not very sure. On the occasion when their child has moved from school to the Centre, they have to come to terms with new faces and new people. Alongside this, of course, is the problem and worry of whether the new changes are going to have any adverse effect on their child. Buildings cannot always be responsible for untoward changes in behaviour, so the people involved become the targets. The anxieties of the parents are mainly concerned with the fact that there has not been time to establish any sort of trusting relationship with the new members of staff. These feelings can manifest themselves in various ways, but one of the most common is that of overprotectiveness towards their child.

Defences have got to be high, and I suppose parents find it hard to say to new members of staff that they don't trust them. But when you have devoted so many years of your life caring so desperately for your child, how can you calmly accept such a major change on behalf of the child without it having an effect on you? So when on the receiving end of a new admission, great thought must be given to these feelings of mistrust. The mistrust is never directed on a personal level. It is part of an overall feeling and is perfectly well justified. Practitioners have not only the responsibility of reassuring the child but also a commitment to relieving the anxieties of the parent. If the parents feel anxious about the situation, then this will be readily and easily transferred to their child. It will then become a mammoth task to cool the situation down. Staff must be able to detach themselves from the mistrust, not take it on board personally, and to see the situation from the viewpoint of the parent. Being aware of the process can go a long way towards rectifying it. Parents will only come to trust staff if the staff can provide the framework for that to happen. Being interested and appearing to care is not enough. Staff have to convey more than that.

Communication is a great instrument in bringing about trustful situations. Parents will become very upset if things are happening or not happening that they ought to know about and do not. Don't forget, they are not expecting great things from the new environment, but they are expecting something. One of the ways in which communication channels can be opened up is by instigating the use of the little black book. A small notebook with a daily record of key points recorded, which can travel with the adult or child, is an excellent method of keeping up-to-date information available for all parties. This is not a time-consuming activity, as only a few lines are needed, as illustrated:

Monday 21st

Susie had a quiet weekend. Sister visited. Watched TV. She came home minus a hat — is it on the unit?

Sending tablets for the week.

Susie's mum

Thanks for tablets. Found the hat — sending it this pm — sorry, Friday afternoon rush.

Susie's had a lovely day. Painting this morning, sat on the patio this afternoon listening to music. Giggled a lot. Ate lunch, shepherd's pie and peas, but wouldn't eat pudding — peaches and cream. Can you send swimming things in for Thursday? Sending home the painting.

Margaret

The painting is lovely. Did she choose the colours herself? Dad was thrilled — it's now on her wall. Susie doesn't like peaches! I'm sending you some tinned fruit for you to keep if situation crops up again. She was worn out when she came home — you must have made her work hard! Can you advise *re* the sore on her back — I'm rather worried. Sending in swimming things — do you want to keep them on the unit, we can always buy another swimsuit for weekends?

Susie's mum

Tuesday 22nd

Thanks for sending in the swimsuit. Yes, it would be better if we could keep it here. She wore it today on the patio. As the weather was nice, we played with the paddling pools and Susie loved it. Had a session with the physio this morning. Noreen says there's definitely improvement on her right side. She's had a bath, and hair washed, and really enjoyed the hair dryer.

We put some lipstick on her and she giggled at herself in the mirror! We've had her back checked, and think it's because of the heat that it looks worse. Sending home some cream which should help, but we're keeping a close eye on it.

By giving details of activities and reactions, the parents are able to get some sort of picture of what is going on. The staff are able to reassure parents of things that might be amiss, like the sore. Just by saying that they are going to keep an eye on it is letting the parents know that the staff are aware of the problem and will monitor it. This improves the start to the trusting process.

AGGRESSION

Aggressive feelings and outbursts can manifest themselves in many different ways. The tendency is to link aggression directly to handicap, and not to see it as a separate issue. To be able to deal with any type of aggressive behaviour we have not only to look at the possible reasons as to why it happened but have also to be aware of our own levels of aggression — and what it means to us.

Perhaps our own fear of aggression is one of our biggest handicaps. Certainly dealing with aggression is something that does not come easily to many. Very often aggression is met with aggression. The normal physiological response is increased adrenalin output — preparing the body for fight or flight. The body is not in a state of calm. It is ready for action. But is the action taken always the right action?

A commonly used method of dealing with aggressive behaviour in handicapped people is to report it. Being able to hand the responsibility over to another party acts as a diffuser to the situation. This other party is usually someone who is also outside of the situation. The offender will be scolded at some point but probably by someone else. This takes away the ill-feeling on the part of the worker. They will not be seen to be handing out the punishment, thereby enabling themselves to save face. This method also reinforces the pecking order and managerial structure. The 'leader' not only carries the responsibility of running the establishment, but also is seen to be a more powerful and authoritative figure — almost as if the worker directly involved is incapable of dealing with the situation. But for the handicapped person though, does it really matter who deals with it? If response is forthcoming anyway, is there any importance held by who will carry it out?

'Reporting' allows a little time for the situation to be assessed. We must try always to be aware of what sets off an aggressive outburst before we can discuss how best to deal with one. Frustration is probably the largest contributing factor. When language communication is a major problem for children and adults, actions very often speak louder than words. Unable to communicate that attention is needed, it is frequently easier to throw something or be abusive. Initially the outburst has the desired effect and attention is drawn. At the time it is probably irrelevant whether the attention is negative or positive. But what constitutes frustration? High on the list must feature boredom, communication problems and dislike.

Case Study

Charlie, a mobile young man of twenty-two years, able to sign key words, able to make sounds but no recognisable speech, arrived one morning in a slightly agitated state. This was a common occurrence, and not one on this particular morning to have caused any unnecessary concern for the staff. He was disruptive throughout the session — crawling over staff, pulling at clothes, obviously upset over something. Charlie had a reputation for frequent displays of attention-seeking behaviour. We asked him dozens of questions in an effort to find out just what was causing his distress. The more time we spent on these questions, the greater his agitation became.

The fruitless results of all this culminated in Charlie rocking quite fiercely and screaming at the top of his voice. He bit his hands, and any others that he could grasp hold of. We were unable to establish the cause of his distress, and all we could do was just ride the storm. What was very clear throughout this episode was that the longer it was taking us to determine the cause, the more frustrated Charlie became. His frustration reached saturation point wherein it turned to aggression.

Having sat and watched this process come about, the frustration levels for the staff involved were at an increased level. I recall that I became so angry myself — with myself. How was it that three members of staff between us could not understand what was going on? This highlighting of our inadequacy obviously added to our own frustration and anger. Our adrenalin levels were up and that energy had to go somewhere. Some of it did spill over onto Charlie and was recognisable by the sheer desperation in our questioning of him, imploring him to give us an answer that we needed to have, in an effort to put right what was wrong.

Needless to say, the effect that all this had on the rest of the group was quite disturbing too. James became so bored with Charlie's takeover of the session that he smacked Ann repeatedly. He also wanted some of the attention, but could not use logical channels to derive it. By being aggressive towards another group member, he knew that we would not be able to ignore it, and have to intercept, which is exactly what we did.

Charlie's friend from the hostel, Martin, also aphasic, at this point started to cry. Martin could not tell us what was wrong. Neither could he enlighten us as to whether the upset was concerning events of the previous evening at home. What we did see was the powerful force behind Charlie's inability to communicate. The group had been completely taken over by Charlie's outburst — including the staff. Other group members had joined in with yet more displays of out-of-character behavioural traits. We admitted defeat, almost as a last resort, both to ourselves and to the group. In a case such as this, we felt that the only course open to us was to give Charlie lots of support and to show him we cared — yet keeping the group cohesive with attention for everyone. Towards the end of the session, Charlie was quite relaxed — all previous signs exhibited had vanished almost entirely.

We later discussed whether this need for attention had been the driving force behind the outburst. Had we been shortsighted in not picking up the signals earlier? As with many similar incidents, one can never know, and can only surmise.

Case Study

Alison had been in the Special Needs Group for twelve months and, although she had had problems with her transition from school, did appear to have settled into the routine. We had worked together for some time and, although the relationship was lacking in terms of our trust of each other, we had seemed to have arrived at a workable arrangement. Without any warning, one morning she attacked me. The outburst was totally unprovoked and later analysis led us to believe that there were no obvious precipitating factors at play. Missiles that were thrown were most definitely directed towards me. Although other staff were in the room, the verbal abuse used contained my name and no one else's. I was the one who came out of it with the bruises and the scratches. The outburst lasted for ten minutes and, as quickly as it started, it finished. The response from staff not involved with this group was quite different to ours. The general feeling was that Alison should be sent home immediately.

Later in the day I approached Alison in an attempt to elicit the cause of the outburst. She went to great lengths to apologise and seemed genuinely concerned over what had happened. I made the point that this was not going to alter my involvement in her activities. If she thought that this was a convenient way of pushing me away, then it was not going to work. In simple terms I told her that if she really did not feel right about a group situation, then if she could tell us, we could do something about it. I acknowledged the fact that there were times when everyone needed to be on their own, and if this was what was upsetting her, then she only had to tell us. I also said that it was difficult to put things right that were wrong when we had no idea when anything was wrong.

We had no way of knowing whether this line of action was appropriate or not. Time may prove this one way or another.

Subsequent sessions, however, were from then on very different. Alison became much closer not only to myself, but to others in the group. She started tentatively to make physical contact with people, which was something she had been unable to do previously. She also laughed much more and a very sharp sense of humour started to emerge. Looking closely at her other reports, it seemed as if she had spent most of her time at school in an isolated way. Her disruptive behaviour had made it difficult for her to be included in various activities. The pattern had long been established and so, when confronted with a reversal of this, she found it hard to feel part of the group process. Built into all this was her insecurity about staff. She really could not trust anyone. Displaying quite obvious antisocial behaviour, reinforced by aggression, was a very big test for the person on the receiving end of it.

Designed to push people away, if anyone could still be prepared to be her friend after all this, then maybe they could be trusted. It was as if she had designed a test for us. How far could we be pushed — and still care?

Some six months following this incident, with a change of staff in the group, the exact same pattern was repeated with another member of staff. Again there were discussions about the appropriate placement of Alison and the 'sending home' syndrome. But in talking to Alison we were pleased to hear her say that she had wanted to be on her own, but she still wanted to be our friend. Would we still love her after this? Although she took drastic steps to establish the ground rules, the results that we have since had make the aggression more than worth the upset caused at the time. Being aggressive may be a crime that at times is not always dealt with, but it certainly is something that does not go unnoticed. If the lifestyle is boring, then aggressive outbursts may be seen as a comforting distractor.

For the severely handicapped child or adult, just how worse can things get? They are deprived of so much as a normal course of events anyway, is there going to be much hardship caused by deprivation of yet more? Some of the punishments that are dealt out may be just exactly what the child wants anyway. Maybe what is wanted is just to go home. They cannot ask to be sent home, but it does not take very long for them to be able to work out just what is needed to bring this about. Being isolated from peers as a punishment may be seen as being an enjoyable punishment. Maybe what is needed is to have the opportunity of being on their own. There is always the watchful eye of someone overseeing every single thing that they do. It is true to say that someone supervises all activities all the time. Even recreation times are supervised. Continually being watched — can we even begin to understand what a lifetime of being watched must feel like?

We know how it feels to have someone looking over our shoulder. This experience is felt by us all at some stage of our lives. But what must it feel like to have this situation with us all the time? We cannot pretend that we would find this state of affairs comfortable, surely? If we recognise the need in ourselves to have some private time, then we ought to recognise it in everyone, including handicapped people.

Taking time out for ourselves is often a way in which we deal with our aggressive traits. Playing sports, gardening, cleaning — just a few of the activities that can accommodate our surplus energy and relieve our stress. Living within the confines of a wheelchair, all activities are dependent on some-one else. For the handicapped, they are entirely at the mercy of others for any diversional activities. Their undisputed lack of choice must be frustrating beyond our comprehension. In our own response to aggression, as I have previously stated, we too become ready for fight or flight. In the instant that it happens our reactions are defensive. This of course is normal. Being aware of danger, we automatically tend to take steps that prevent accidents occurring and damage being done. Un-fortunately we make little allowance for hearing the other side of the story. We pay token attention to what happens before an outburst and all too often fail to recognise the cause.

What often does happen is that there seems to be an immediate urge to tidy things up so that normal service can be resumed as soon as possible. Suppressing the situation, often interpreted as dealing with it, might be seen to be a logical move for staff, but it is rarely logical for the handi-capped person. The conflict may appear to be resolved, but in most cases it is not. Having used up energy to create the disturbance, afterwards the person may appear to be quiet and settled. In a way the outburst has been therapeutic. The tension has been relieved. The underlying cause in what prompted it in the first place, though, is rarely found. This will inevitably result in repercussions at some later stage.

The longer-term effects of this are that the handicapped person will become easily labelled as being 'difficult', 'danger-ous', 'unpredictable'. One of the spin-offs of this is that staff's views will become clouded. There will be a hesitancy on their part when having to work with someone with a history of aggression, raising anxiety levels for both parties, and being a prime cause for a repeat performance. Being aggressive is an expression of feeling and emotion. It is our responsibility to do all we can to find the answers and not to be content with just merely tidying things up. To do this means that we must look critically at our own behaviour, as well as that of those in our care.

It may be that we are the provokers of aggression. We may not be doing this deliberately, or even consciously, but nevertheless we must be honest enough to admit to this being a possibility. Were we rushing things along too quickly? Was our spoken word inappropriate? Were our expectations too high? Were they too low? The questions are endless, but they must be asked. In trying to establish what offsets behavioural disturbances, we must be ever aware of all possibilities. It is too easy to jump to the wrong conclusions and put it all down to 'the handicap'. It might very well be that 'the handicap' is the cause — but surely not just on it's own? It is not a failing to admit to making a mistake — especially if the mistake gives us a possible answer to the problem. But it is a failing if we cannot be honest. We can make a start by recognising the aggression within ourselves — painful though it may be.

LANGUAGE

The essence of communication is the ability to do it. Use of language is the method we most commonly employ in our daily transactions. Our body language communicates things we leave unspoken. Having the use of limbs, when speech is not possible due to physical complications, we can gesticulate and write what we want to say. Signing, for those familiar with the skill, provides a means of communication that is fast and effective.

The problem for children and adults in Special Care Units is that, for many, language is not accessible and movement of limbs is impossible — the reality being that signing is also out of reach for this particular group. I am not suggesting that, because a child or adult is handicapped, then no attempt ought to be made to introduce signing. But there are times when we have simply to acknowledge that there are people in our care who will never be able to use these systems. It is on this category that I wish to concentrate here.

When a baby begins to use sounds, there is a tendency on the part of parents, families and others to use baby talk. This is something that I personally find quite disturbing. I cannot understand how energy can be spent encouraging a child to say 'bow wow' when 'dog' is much shorter and much simpler.

Similarly, 'moo cow', 'choo choo train', 'pussy' are all words whose use is frequently encouraged.

When a child begins to develop vocabulary, the emphasis is then switched and they are actively discouraged from using these initial phrases. 'You're a big boy now. Big boys don't say "choo choo train", they say "train".' How confusing this must be for the child. They must have some wonderful ideas about what makes adults tick, if the messages we give them change so drastically in a relatively short space of time.

The development of the child dictates the change in choice of vocabulary, and this is primarily instigated by parents. For a handicapped child, where development is very slow or (as is often the case) just does not happen at all, there is the tendency always to regard the child as a child, even if that child happens to be over twenty-one years of age. We would be surprised if an adult used words such as 'bow wow' and 'choo choo train', but we find this quite acceptable if the adult is functioning on four-year-old standards. Parents of a normal child start to encourage the change of language — with a handicapped child, they do not. It is as if they are so pleased with the ability to use any words at all that they somehow never seem to see the need for progress with the actual choice of words used. By reinforcing the babyish phrases, they are reinforcing the baby in the child. To take this to extremes, they are actually depriving the child of normal language development.

We acquire words by listening to and copying words that are spoken to us — the vast majority of which come from adults. But if the handicapped child is only hearing baby talk, then baby talk is what they will acquire. The repercussions of this are immeasurable. One factor worth considering is that when *we* use baby talk, we tend to use a different tone of voice than we would if we were speaking ordinarily. We also tend to expect a baby reaction to what we are saying. Inevitably if we are adopting this babyish way, is it any wonder that these children never grow up!

The handicapped child will soon begin to grasp the idea that the language chosen for them and the language used for others are completely different. Not only are the words different, but the tone and pace of voice used are also different. Will this make them feel different? I would argue that it will.

This whole area of language is one that interests me greatly, and I feel that it is something to which we pay little attention. It is easy to forget that the vocabulary of profoundly handicapped people does not extend to our own. We take for granted that, when we say something, it is understood. In more cases than not, it isn't.

On analysis it often occurs that, when directing a statement, we tend to back it up with some visual clue. There may not be a comprehension of the word, but the visual back-up helps to interpret what was said and, in most cases, people can take a guess and hope that it's right. Very few handicapped people will admit to not understanding what you have said. Because they don't question you, you must never presume that they are always in tune with what it is you are saying. For the handicapped child who has no speech, the world becomes a much smaller place. We have no way of knowing if they understand what we are saying, unless we ask something direct and it is followed by the prescribed response.

It is difficult to conduct one-way conversations. When we talk to someone we usually hold eye contact, and there is always some acknowledgement of the fact that we are speaking. With profoundly handicapped people, they may be unable to hold eye contact. They may not give out any signals that there is an acknowledgement of us speaking at all. This makes it very off-putting for the speaker. How long can you keep up a conversation without getting any reaction at all? If there is no indication that what you are talking about is relevant, interesting or amusing, without signals how do you continue? I find that the hardest task is to pace what is being said. On a one-to-one basis, if the person is slow to respond, there is not the same degree of urgency that there is in a group setting. If there are just the two of you, it does not matter that you may not get a reply for ten minutes. But if the group are involved in an activity, then there is not the time to be able to sit back and just wait. Other group members need group time too and we cannot afford the luxury of spending time with just one person to the exclusion of everyone else. Pressure of time is probably the biggest enemy in any language development programme.

Having articulate members of the group alongside aphasic members has advantages and disadvantages. The chattering from peers often helps as a stimulator for the others to speak, but it can also act as a deterrent. Aphasic people may feel unsure about attempting to speak if they feel that other speakers are overpowering. The other problem here is that, when asking one of the lesser speaking members a question that you think may get a response from them, before they have time to take a breath, the speakers shout out the answer, thereby reinforcing the hesitancy.

As practitioners we may feel that there are times when what we say produces no response at all — therefore we believe that our spoken word has not been understood. But how many times have we heard the stilted sounds — not necessarily words, just sounds — of those in our care and been equally unresponsive ourselves? We use our own vocabulary base, and expect others to meet our demands, all at a very subconscious level. Shouldn't we perhaps be a little more flexible? We can continue to teach our language, but at the same time be more open-minded about the language that handicapped people use for us. We are much better equipped than they to make any adaptions necessary.

I often wonder about the increased frustration levels that arise out of communication difficulties. I know I have contributed to the stress — because I have not been able to understand. I know that on occasions when I have stopped using speech, the stress has been minimised. By being aware of our actions, and carefully and accurately noting the responses that they incur, we can then begin to be more selective about why and when we choose to use the spoken word. The value comes in not simply being able to teach vocabulary — but also in knowing when it is time to keep quiet and shut up.

3   Complicating Handicap

It's Got Nothing to Do With Handicap

Mental handicap is always seen as being *the* problem first and foremost, and psychiatric complications are simply an extension of the handicap. In the majority of cases the mental handicap is obvious whereas the mental illness is not. It is very easy to dismiss other aspects of the person if they have the burden of a handicap. Strange behavioural traits are seen to be part of the handicapped process. Although we must acknowledge that handicap contributes to other areas of difficulty, we must be ever aware of other causes — causes outside of the handicap itself. It can be difficult and at times impossible to separate the handicap. I am not suggesting that we ignore it completely, merely that we should not be so hasty in jumping to some of the conclusions that we tend to make. If we believe that one in three people will suffer from some form of mental illness in their lifetime, then handicapped people too will be at risk.

It can be argued that some of the stresses and strains of everyday life will not touch handicapped people in the community — the stresses of high-powered occupations or problems of running a home and budgeting. Because their lives take different paths from our own, this does not mean that they will be immune from psychiatric problems. Being safe within a caring environment is no preventative cure for psychiatric disorder.

DEPRESSION

Things that happen to cause us great sadness and loss inevitably result in changed behaviour on our part. We react to the situation. We are aware of the process and, if unable to deal with it ourselves, can be offered the services of trained personnel within the field. Sleep patterns may be disrupted. We may suffer insomnia, early morning wakening, loss of appetite, lethargy, general slowing up, poor concentration, apathy, indifference, no energy or interest in people or environment — the list is endless. With powers of rationale and logic, we are able to recognise these abnormal feelings. In cases where we can't, then someone who is close to us will. In any event, the situation is rarely allowed to deteriorate without intervention of one kind or another. For the handicapped child, to struggle through life ordinarily is difficult enough, but to have to live with depression must be quite intolerable.

Without our full quota of sleep we become irritable. We can say that we are like this because we are not sleeping well and our actions are then excusable. The uncommunicative child cannot do this. If we have loss of appetite and choose not to eat, or make do with a snack, this is acceptable. We are not going to fade away if we skip the occasional meal. The profoundly handicapped child has no choice. Food is shovelled in whether they want it or not. 'To build them up.' 'They need the nourishment.' This is very often the last thing that they need. Not having the luxury of choice, it must feel awful to be 'force-fed'. How would we react if we were being made to eat when we did not want to?

We will never know to what extent depressive illness affects severely handicapped children and adults. We can only try to be aware of tell-tale signs. The signs have got to be seen as being *independent* of the handicap and not part of it. Of course, the two things are very closely linked. For profoundly handicapped people, continually having to deal with practitioners around them, interfering with what they want and don't want, twenty-four hours each day, must be a major contributing factor to irritability and depression. Sitting in an uncomfortable position for long periods of time, and boredom, must also play a part in this process. Boredom feeds

restlessness and irritability. It has this effect on non-handicapped sections of the community, so severely handicapped
people cannot be seen as being immune to these processes.
The contributing causes must never be underestimated.

DEALING WITH OR TREATING OR BOTH?

We must ask ourselves if we would do something about it if
someone close to us was depressed? Of course we would.
Let's take this as a starting point.

In our daily lives we are confronted by depression in someone close to us — and we suffer it ourselves. It is hardly a
condition that we can ignore. We are all prone to having off
days, the days when nothing ever seems to go right. Sometimes the reasons are quite silly and trivial — but the effects
that they can have on us are seldom seen in the same way.
How we deal with off days is as diverse as the reasons for
having them. If the situation develops whereby it is obvious
that what is wrong is far more than just an off day, then steps
are taken to put things right.

What I would like to know is, if we can see this pattern
emerging so clearly in ourselves and those we work and live
with, why don't we see it in handicapped people? We certainly
would not ignore depression in someone who did not have a
handicap. My belief is that when we see handicap we see very
little else. The first thing we must do before we can begin to
deal with depression, or even treat it, is to acknowledge and
establish that it could be there. To be able to do that we
must be able to see it. To be able to see it we must be aware
of what it is that we are looking for. By recognising the process we can do an awful lot to make things better.

Comfort is a wonderful thing. A shoulder to cry on and a
sympathetic ear are sometimes the very things that we need
to make things better. We are able to seek these out for ourselves — but what of the handicapped adult? Are they in a
position to do this? Being off your food, you would certainly
not thank someone for putting a huge plate of meat and
three veg. in front of you, now would you? By exercising
only a small amount of commonsense, you are able to diffuse

the situation and not make matters worse.

Where communication is difficult or impossible, it is your eyes and ears that are going to be the deciding factor in the mental welfare of the handicapped person. If it is obvious that all your tender loving care is not making the slightest difference to the situation, then it might be sensible to ask the advice of an appropriate agency — GP, Social Worker, Consultant and so on.

Depression is not cured by comfort alone. If the symptoms are severe, then it may well be that a course of antidepressants could be the answer. Remember that handicapped people cannot refer themselves. It is up to the people who are on the spot to do something — in effect, you. Electroconvulsive therapy, antidepressants, counselling and therapy are recognised treatments for depression. They are not solely treatments for 'normal' people. They are treatments used appropriately to prevent suffering and enable people to get back to their normal lives as soon as possible. The handicapped person has as much right to them as anyone else. Bearing in mind that their lifestyle is far more depressing than anyone else's anyway, they should be a priority. It is up to you to ensure that priority.

OBSESSIONAL TRAITS

Without even thinking about it, we all build into our lives a pattern of obsessional traits that are difficult and/or impossible to change. Some common examples are:

Which side of the bed we sleep on.

Which sock we put on first — left or right.

Which arm we put into the sleeve of a shirt first — left or right.

Which foot we start a flight of stairs on.

and so on.

A lot of everyday actions are determined by right or left dominance factors, but setting this apart, we still have many rituals that we stick to quite rigidly. Only when these rituals begin to interfere with other patterns of our lifestyle are they interpreted as being serious or 'obsessional'.

Case Study

Brenda always took her shoes off before she started working with me. It took on average some ten minutes from taking them off to actually starting work. She went through quite a lengthy ritual of measuring them together, then placing them side by side at the edge of the mat. She changed their position at least twenty times before she was able to sit down with me. Once sitting next to me, she then changed them round again. Fractions of an inch were important to her, and until they were in the exact position, we were unable to do any work at all. If another person was working in the same area at the same time, she would then repeat this process with their shoes, and then mine. Sometimes this process was so time-consuming that by the time she had finished rearranging all the shoes, the session was over.

A happy compromise seemed to be asking her to arrange all the shoes half an hour in advance of her session. Acknowledging her need for ritual was far more therapeutic than trying to change it. Her anxiety levels were much lower for being able to do this. On the occasions when we tried to prevent her from doing it, she became so agitated that we were unable to do any work together at all. Recognising her need for tidiness did not seem to be detrimental to the running of the Unit. In fact, she managed to change some of our less obsessional ways! Great uniformity was apparent when Brenda helped us to set tables, tidying up our place settings.

Hand washing and hand wringing are common anxiety and obsessional traits. Never forget, if we raise our own anxiety levels by trying to stop them, then we in turn will only aggravate the situation. Obsessional neurosis is not part of a diagnostic procedure for establishing the type or degree of handicap, so it should never be classified as such. It is a separate issue that should be dealt with separately. Obsessions are fairly deep-rooted and have usually developed over a period of time. It is therefore safe to assume that they are hardly going to disappear overnight. It is difficult to generalise, as all individual cases vary so considerably. The important thing to remember is that we are to employ whatever it takes not to aggravate the situation further — and be flexible and adaptable in our approach.

Case Study

Joyce was involved in the swimming programme. She was able to dress and undress with help. On arrival at the pool she proceeded to go through lengthy rituals before she was ready for her swim. Methodically undressing and placing each item of clothing in her prescribed way took ages. Everything had to be folded into four: it was then placed in a special way on the bench; it was then folded into two piles. Her socks were individually shaken, then folded carefully and placed into her shoes. She then placed the shoes in the rack under the pile of clothes. Then she moved her hat, coat and scarf from the original peg and placed them over the peg that corresponded with her clothes. When all that was done she took her towel (carefully folded) and her hat and slowly walked towards the mirror. When every strand of hair was in the right position, she slowly took her hat and very carefully put it on. More adjustments were made to her hair and, picking up her towel and rechecking her appearance, she was ready.

By the time she got to the poolside and folded her towel on one of the chairs, it was time for the group to get out of the water and get changed! They had all had half an hour water time and Joyce hadn't had any. The ritual for getting dressed was as lengthy and laborious. It drove us mad! Nothing anyone could say or do made the slightest bit of difference. There was no way we were ever going to change the habits of a lifetime.

The ritual was more important to Joyce than the activity. She wanted to go swimming — but not at the expense of having to change her patterns. For those of us who throw clothes on in any old fashion, having this sort of obsession is hard to deal with because it is so alien to us. Joyce was clearly not going to give in to group pressure — or any other pressure. Her obsessional ways were the priority. If any changes were going to happen, then we were the people who would have to make them.

On her third visit to the pool, I made sure that she arrived with the group that preceded her group — and returned with the group that followed. This meant that she could continue at her own pace with her obsessions — still have half an hour water time — and then change again at her own pace. The object of the exercise was that Joyce actually got into the water. Changing our routine seemed a small price to pay.

Case Study

Colin enjoyed participating in all activities. He was always keen and enthusiastic and often volunteered to 'go first'. Unfortunately before he could actually do anything, he had a series of ritualistic mannerisms that he had to do. First of all he would straighten out all his clothing. This could take up to ten minutes. Then he counted to twenty and before he could go any further he recited the following: 'Right. OK. You can do it. Yes I can. OK. Right. Now.' When all this was done he would take a big breath and go and get the chair, or whatever it was that he had been asked to do. More often than not I had forgotten what it was I had asked him as I had to wait so long for him to do it!

No amount of encouragement or cajoling made any difference. The rest of the group would become irritated and this clearly upset him. It was obvious that he was distressed by his obsessive behaviour, but was unable to do anything about it. To try and resolve his conflict I structured his obsessions. By organising the rest of the group, it was easy to accommodate Colin. He had great satisfaction in being the first to be asked to do something. This did not necessarily mean that he always wanted to be first to do it. So I simply asked him first, followed by 'a bit later Colin, please, if you can', and it worked every time. The rest of the group were able to get on with things and Colin was pleased that he was doing what was asked of him. Once I had been able to provide a clearer structure for him, he felt better able to participate.

ANXIETY STATES

Rational or irrational fear raises pulse rates, increases adrenalin output and frequency of micturition, makes the skin clammy and causes distress — along with a never-ending list of other symptoms. If we are unaware of what is going to happen to us, we become anxious. With handicapped people there is a tendency not to explain what is going to happen to them, and an even greater tendency just to do things suddenly and without warning.

Changes to routine and environment cause anxiety, and anything we can do to relieve this stress can only be in everyone's best interests. We know ourselves how we feel when we become anxious about something: sitting a driving test, having an interview, taking an exam, and so on. The symptoms not only affect the situation we find ourselves in at the time, but also spread over into other areas of our lives. We may lie awake at night worrying over something, or wake early in the morning thinking about the problem. If we are seriously troubled then we may tend to lose our concentration and not hear things that are said to us. We may not pay enough attention to what we are dealing with — the probabilities are endless. The point I am trying to make is that if anxiety affects *us* in this way, then it is going to have the very same effects on handicapped people too.

DEALING WITH ANXIETY

There are a number of ways that we can deal with the problem. We can do an awful lot in the preventative sense. If we are the cause of the anxiety in the first place, then we really must try to do something about our own behaviour. We must be careful that we do not create the circumstances that provoke anxious situations for those in our care. Stress is a major contributing factor to anxiety. We will only feed the anxiety if we maintain stressful situations. A little bit of 'think before you do' ought to be the rule here.

However, there are situations that develop for which we are not responsible. The anxiety levels are raised by other factors and we have to try to devise ways of reducing them. Relaxation and massage are extremely useful 'cures'. There is no excuse for not using them. Gentle soothing, stroking of arms, legs, backs, necks, shoulders, is sometimes all that is needed to take the stress away. Finger massage is wonderful if done with hand cream. Getting results with foot massage depends on the 'tickling threshold' but is well worth trying. By introducing physical contact you are facilitating a closeness that creates a feeling of special attention being given. The attention alone may be all that is needed. Whispering or talking quietly is a great diffuser of anxiety and reassurance ought to be given.

If all that fails and it seems that the anxiety is beyond the help you can offer, then rally round the appropriate help of someone who can do something. It isn't a failing to admit that you don't know what to do. But don't sit back and allow the situation to worsen — go and find someone who can do something.

MANIC STATES

These are defined as spasmodic/periodical alterations in mood, as opposed to constant hyperactivity. Excitable mood swings, overt happiness and hyperactivity can be as painful to the individual as the depths of depression. In creating happy atmospheres, there must be an awareness of mood changes. A person in a manic state will present as being extremely overactive. Thought processes are so rapid that by the time the words actually come out of the mouth, they have changed from their original format and the brain is already working on the next dozen sentences. Speech becomes disjointed, jumping from one subject to the next without any apparent connection to the listener. There is inability to sit still — in fact a general speeding up of all processes. Concentration spans are poor, and it is impossible for the person to complete anything that is started.

This picture represents the type of behaviour very often seen with handicapped people and it must not automatically be seen as being attributable to the handicap and nothing else.

DEALING WITH MANIA

I have always had a bit of a soft spot for manic patients. I know from my own experiences that I much prefer elevation of mood as opposed to being miserable. There is something quite splendid about feeling on top of the world — and we all tend to make the most of it when it occurs. The realities of life unfortunately do not always allow this feeling to last for very long. But while it is happening we are confident and energetic. We feel able to be more active — we want to do something active. If we can recognise these qualities in handicapped people, then we must endeavour to create situations that can accommodate their moods.

It makes little sense to think that, because we are program-
med to 'tell stories' at 3 pm and discover that the groups are
elated, we should go ahead and stick to the original plan. Just
because it is on the programme shouldn't always be the
proviso for doing it. If the group are happy and boisterous —
then channel it positively. Use the raised confidence levels to
do some of the things that they find difficult. I have found
that people who have problems with balance (unsure about
lifting feet off the floor, for example) will when elated have a
much more positive attitude towards the activity. Of course
when you have been able to get them to do it once, you are
well on the way to being able to encourage them to do it
again. Don't throw your arms up and despair at the mania —
go along with it and use it to your advantage. There's nothing
like a manic patient to brighten up the day!

NEUROLOGICAL/ORGANIC TOXIC STATES

This is far too complex a subject to be covered in a book of
this nature. As with other areas of psychiatry, it has been
expertly dealt with by specialists in the field. My inclusion
here is to remind the reader that changing patterns of behaviour when seen with handicapped people can often be
brought about by one of the above. A common precipitating
factor to changed behaviour is 'drugs'.

We need to be aware of all medication that is being taken
— whether we are responsible for the dispensing or not. Also
we need to be fully aware of any contraindications. There is
not much point in giving someone an aspirin to relieve a
headache if the side effects are going to be disastrous. If
handicapped people in our care display behaviour that is felt
to be 'not normal' or out of character, then we must be
sufficiently open enough in our observations to consider all
possible causes and ask for advice.

SCHIZOPHRENIA

In 1970 a tutor told me that I could call myself a nurse when
I could smell schizophrenia! All these years later I feel further
away from understanding schizophrenia now than I ever did

then. In many ways I am reluctant to include a section on schizophrenia and am only doing so to share some of my experiences. The reader must decide if the people referred to really are schizophrenics.

Schizophrenia is an ill-defined illness and in many ways a nonentity. The medical profession disagree on many aspects, and descriptions and criteria vary enormously. The main types include simple, hebephrenic, paranoid and catatonic.

Without the never-ending debate on what schizophrenia is, without any mention of the apathy, poor concentration spans, poor relationships, delusions and the host of other so-called symptoms that collectively gathered may constitute the correct diagnosis, I wish to concentrate on just one aspect — hallucinations. I realise that they too are debatable. However, I refer to auditory hallucinations and my intent is to try to separate them from handicap.

For the person who is hallucinating, the voice heard inside their head is far more real than yours or mine. It is very difficult to be in competition with something knowing that you can never win before you even start. It is like being asked to whisper a message just as alarm bells start ringing. The bells would be heard — the whispering would not. Wouldn't it be better to wait until the bells stop ringing before whispering? Wouldn't there be a better chance of being heard? If practitioners feel that there is a possibility that the handicapped person may be hallucinating, by joining in the competition to demand attention (which is exactly what happens) only adds to the confusion. Getting annoyed and irritated is certainly not going to make the situation any easier.

We might be convinced that concentration is poor if we are unable to attract attention and unable to hold it. But concentration may be good, and may be held by voices other than ours. Because we tend to associate things like poor concentration spans to handicap, we then shut our eyes to other wider possibilities. Voices chattering away could be engaged in quite harmless conversation — almost pleasant even. But it is not beyond the realms of possibility that the voices are telling people to do dreadful things. Hallucinations are not divorced from abusive language and antisocial behaviour. Complying with the forceful demands given inside their heads, schizophrenics can be made to do almost anything. Without any understanding of this process, the practitioner can easily be drawn into making statements about the person that are not correct. An example might be 'refused to get dressed' or 'refused to eat breakfast'. In fact it is quite likely that they did not refuse anything at all. If the voices have told them to leave food and clothes alone, then they would have been obeying these orders. Working with the hallucinations is far better than appearing to be working against them.

Schizophrenia might be many things to many people, but one thing it most certainly is, is devastating. The torment that can become a way of life is as disabling as any handicap. But the more profound the handicap, the greater the difficulty to diagnose. Floridly psychotic people can be extremely disruptive to any situation. In many ways, their behaviour prevents their inclusion in group activities — for all the wrong reasons.

Case Study

John is very stubborn and refuses to go on any outings. He has a label of being 'difficult'. John's voices tell him constantly that if he goes outside then awful things will happen to him. His reluctance to go anywhere is quite understandable. Unfortunately his mental handicap — not his schizophrenia — determines his type of care. Seeing John for the first time his handicap is obvious, whereas his schizophrenia is not.

My own experiences have brought me into contact with many mentally handicapped schizophrenics who have been treated very successfully with long-acting phenothiazines. I am not one for advocating the use of drugs as the cure for all ills, but as an alternative to the disabling symptoms that schizophrenia can cause, then I would recommend their use. If they can be prescribed to stop the torment then quality of life can be greatly improved. But drugs are never the be all and end all in the treatment of psychiatric illness. An understanding of the process and insight into what's going on go an awful long way to preventing further distress.

THE FEAR OF MENTAL ILLNESS

As with handicap, there is still tremendous ignorance and lack of understanding of psychiatric disorders. Asking parents to cope with handicap is one thing — asking them to cope with a psychiatric disturbance as well is often too much. Nothing grieves me more than seeing parents refusing treatment for their child. Even when they are fully informed of the circumstances and the difficulties, they can still bring themselves to deny their child a treatment that will improve quality of life.

In normal circumstances, a young adult of twenty suffering from a psychotic breakdown would have all the help, support and encouragement possible from the family. The family would be the key figures in ensuring that medication was taken — to keep the dreadful symptoms at bay. To prevent their son or daughter from suffering further, they would do all they could and cooperate with whatever agency was involved to bring a halt to the suffering. But this is not so with a handicapped adult. Refusing to believe that their son or daughter has a psychiatric disturbance, they endeavour to treat it themselves — at home. Obviously this is not always the case, but it does happen with alarming frequency. So despite our observations and speedy referrals, we are at times quite helpless. But sadly, because of handicap, mental illness is often never treated.

To conclude this section, I think it can be summed up very simply by a few golden rules:

(i)   Be aware of factors beyond the handicap.
(ii) Exercise commonsense.
(iii) Don't prolong the agony by accepting handicap as an umbrella.
(iv) Do something about it — today.
(v)   If you can't, then find someone who can.

IT'S PHYSICAL — NOT MENTAL

There seems to be something strange happening when it comes to nursing or caring for profoundly handicapped people. We are all very aware of how profound the handicap actually is, but the severity of the handicap somehow blocks our vision to so many other things. It is almost as if we believe that profound handicap is enough — with disabilities such as incontinence, immobility and aphasia, what possible further complications could there be? Mental handicap unfortunately is not an immunity for other complications. We know that we cannot expect to spend our own lifetimes completely free of physical illness and so the same must be said of profoundly handicapped people too.

There is within us all an ongoing degenerative process. As we get older we almost expect to suffer from a variety of complaints and complications. Profoundly handicapped people are no different. Their handicap is not a protective force that keeps other illnesses at bay. We have the luxury of being able to reach for the pain killers or seek advice — handicapped people do not. The profoundly handicapped child or adult is entirely at the mercy of others for picking up the signals that something may be wrong. In looking after that child or adult, we must be aware of all the possible reasons for things going wrong. It is never enough simply to say 'it's because they're handicapped'.

To start to list the possible complications that could occur would warrant another book. By keeping this section brief, however, the reader is not to presume that this in any way detracts from the importance I place on this crucial aspect of care. As mentioned throughout, I am endeavouring to go beyond the handicap. Yes, handicap may be the primary cause for many variables in health — but it is certainly not the contributing factor to all.

Basic nursing care can sometimes be so basic that even the most normal aspects of health care are overlooked. It is easy to say that it is up to practitioners to have an awareness of the physical signals that may be given out — but none of us can be aware if we do not allow ourselves to be receptive and open to the possibilities that could arise. Nourishing, well balanced diets may be available, but unless the feeding regime is effective then the best diet in the world will prove to be useless and futile. Actually to fulfil commitments of providing good standards of basic care, we must first of all look at the standards we set for ourselves. If we set double standards, then is this fair? When I nursed on a geriatric ward, I often used to ask myself if the standards maintained would be good enough for members of my family. All too often the answer was no. The same applies to handicap. If standards are not good enough for a member of your own family, then they are not good enough for anyone else.

HANDICAP – THE BEST EXCUSE OF ALL

The term 'handicap' becomes the umbrella under which all manner of symptoms present themselves. We pay little attention to physical and psychological problems that, although at times are directly attributable to the handicap, are nevertheless quite separate issues from it. It is almost as if the power of the 'handicap' label prevents us from seeing other aspects. Even when we do eventually recognise the separate symptoms, we tend to attach minimal importance to them.

As professionals we are prejudiced in our modes of treatment. Were similar symptoms presented by normal children and adults, action would be taken immediately. The power of handicap influences us to such a degree that we unknowingly tend not to refer and tend not to treat. The restrictions of our Health Service limits treatment where it is needed most. Hospital and Outpatient Departments function on long waiting lists. Priority patients are seen first and everyone else has to wait.

For many handicapped people, symptoms are not picked up in the early stages of illness, simply because the practitioners fail to recognise that symptoms are in effect present. Too hastily we ignore warning signs, and then find ourselves in a situation whereby emergency treatment is needed. By this time the handicapped person has suffered pain and discomfort for a much longer period of time than would be tolerated by ourselves. Very often we can do something positive about physical complications and issues that are separate from handicap, if only we would allow ourselves to be aware of them.

Labelling

We attach labels as a means of identifying the price or contents of something. The label in effect indicates the value or the worth.

HANDICAP

Handicap as a label immediately tells us that the person in question is not normal. There is something missing or something not quite right. Our responses to a handicapped person are very different from the responses we would make were the person non-handicapped. Irrespective of the type or degree of handicap, we somehow cannot respond in a normal way. The person who has the handicap is instantly at a disadvantage — not from any of their difficulties, but from ours. We use the label all too often as a rationale for a change in our behaviour.

BEHAVIOUR

If we think about how we use labels to define behaviour, we can easily justify our responses to that behaviour.

As a child I remember an old lady who lived at the end of the road. She terrorised us by brandishing her walking stick every time we played within ten yards of her house. Her label was one of being mad and dangerous. That was enough reason to keep out of her way. But the truth of the matter was that she was not mad at all and she certainly was not dangerous. We terrified her. To keep us at a distance she adopted the behaviour described. Unfortunately, because she acquired the label in these circumstances for this particular situation, the label was attached to other aspects of her life. This sort of thing happens to us all the time. A one-off situation, given enough attention, can give us a label we may never be able to lose. To admit to locking oneself out of the house or car is fatal. The reputation for doing this sort of thing all the time will very quickly develop, without any real justification at all. 'Once' does not mean 'always.'

JARGON

We seem to have an uncontrollable compulsion to use long-winded explanations and technical terminology to explain the simplest of things. We take the basis of language and change it into an almost unrecognisable form. By borrowing bits from other languages and inventing new words, we then use this new language without giving a second thought to any consideration of the language being accessible to others or not.

Jargon, for some unknown reason, seems to impress. It is almost as if we do not need to know what it actually means — we just need to be able to hear it and speak it. But who uses it? We all use it. Wrapped up in our own way of explaining things, we easily resort to jargon and labels applicable to our backgrounds and training. Different disciplines make use of different terminology, but the end result is the same. We too freely attach labels that are never removed.

IS IT REALLY NECESSARY?

What we must ask ourselves is why we use it? Do we need to use jargon to convey what it is we want to say? Can we say the same thing without using technical terminology? The most complex of explanations can be written and spoken about in simplistic forms. So why do we use jargon? We use it to retain our credibility on a professional basis. As professionals it is expected of us by others that we are able to baffle people by our knowledge. The best way to baffle others is to talk to them on a level that is beyond their comprehension. The best tool to use is jargon.

Professionals are the biggest offenders. Specialist fields of training are full of language that is almost exclusive to that particular subject area. Nurses are encouraged to write that the patient had 'epistaxis' when nose bleed would suffice. By complicating the language, we are almost instigating a superiority over others. Do we really need this power?

The power of a label is easily transferrable to others. Just because someone had one aggressive outburst, due to the frustration of not being able to convey what it was that was needed at the time, the aggressive tag becomes part of their life. It does not take long for that person to work out that aggressive behaviour is going to promote response. It may not be the response that is desired, but it is a response nonetheless.

By labelling, we are in effect perpetuating the very behaviour that we find undesirable. If we were better able to deal with the situations as they arise, in the context of their surroundings, we might very well find that this would stop us using labels as the excuse for overall unacceptable behavioural patterns. Labels become pegs on which we can hang things. They are the excuse for occurrences to which we need to apportion blame.

A parent once said 'Johnny can't help it, he's Down's syndrome, you know.' The label is the acceptable excuse for behaviour that normally would not be tolerated. We capitalise on labels and jargon. We use them to the full. They are the excuses, they are the blame, they are the reasons we employ for our logic and rationale. We must remember though that the handicapped person uses them too.

Case Study

Barbara, thirty years of age, had been involved in a number of incidents of aggressive behaviour and there was considerable concern over the unpredictable and dangerous outbursts of this young lady. In counselling, Barbara said she couldn't help it. When we explored some of the reasons for her aggressive behaviour, her parents had told her that it was because she was handicapped and therefore it was not her fault. The label of handicap became the excuse for almost anything she wanted to do. The label removed her boundaries and sense of direction, and without both of these, her behaviour became uncontrollable. The double set of standards of play — those of her parents and those of the staff — made the situation very difficult for everyone concerned.

THE VALUE OF JARGON AND LABELLING

While it can be argued against, there is also a very good case for the appropriate use of labels. Diagnosis is never simple and in most cases is technical. However, what is written into case notes is written in medical terminology, and, difficult though it may be for some of us, it is an inevitable fact of life. Correct diagnosis is important, as this will determine the future of the child. The diagnosis that is made will very much determine the machinery that is put into operation, which will involve other disciplines. Clear and concise facts are necessary for everyone involved to be able to make their own assessments. Basic things need to be established very early on in the proceedings. Specialist equipment may need to be ordered and, without specific information, mistakes can be made.

Apart from equipment, there may be other factors to be considered. Medication, clothing, diet, posture, physiotherapy and so on. Inevitably jargon will be used and it needs to be understood so that everyone involved with the child or adult is aware of all implications. In their dealings with each other, the professionals ought to have an understanding of the language used. They are going to be the people who will put treatment plans and care plans into operation effectively. But the care of the profoundly handicapped person goes beyond the professionals. The families and friends and voluntary agencies involved with the child or adult must be aware of the information that is passing from one professional to the other. It is up to all of us to make sure that everyone has the facts.

It must be very confusing for parents to have a lot of words thrown at them without back-up explanations. There are ways of explaining things and ways of explaining things. A little bit of thought will enable us to tone down the complexity of the terminology used and enable us to present it in a more accessible form. It must be remembered that we are working towards providing a better quality of life for the handicapped person. We can only achieve this if we are all working together. It serves no purpose to keep the technical side of things to ourselves. Because we acquired the information in a complicated way does not mean that it has to stay that way. Are we so inflexible that we cannot change the language to suit the situation?

It is very easy to get lost within our jargon. In our search to answer questions and come to terms with why things are as they are, we fall back on technicalities. It is almost as if by finding the peg to hang things on we can resolve the problem. I would never underestimate the value of being able to isolate a problem and deal with it appropriately, as long as we are able to do this objectively. But as long as we continue to cloud everything under the 'umbrella' term of handicap, unable to see other factors that are equally and at times more important issues than just the handicap, then we will never be able to see the handicapped child as a person in their own right.

Yes, it is important to know that someone has cerebral palsy or Hurler's syndrome or Down's syndrome — but it will not be very beneficial to know the diagnosis and not be able to get beyond the label and find the person. So many profoundly handicapped people have such complicated aspects of condition that very often it is impossible to distinguish one from the other. No two people are alike. We are, each of us, individual with our own personalities and our own ways. Profoundly handicapped people in our care are no different.

We must never allow the label to dictate the prescription for care. We must take it into account by all means, but not to the exclusion of everything else. A sense of perspective is what is needed. The ability to use and understand jargon selectively and yet retain objectivity towards care is essential.

Recording, Monitoring, Charting

ASSESSMENT

It is my intention here to discuss the value of recording information, rather than select specific formats already in operation. I always find that assessment forms and procedures are all very well, but they never seem to cover all the areas that are applicable to my particular situation. Like the majority of questionnaires, the questions are nearly appropriate, but never exact. In selecting an answer, I find that I am not really presenting a true and honest picture — merely one that is nearly right. Unless you have the opportunity of working with the child from a very early age, it almost goes without saying that someone, at some time, will have completed some form of assessment, or written some notes, before you begin your work. In all fields there are standard procedure forms to be completed for admission. They ask for standard replies in

a standard format — leaving space at the end for 'other information'.

CASE NOTES

Whether the child is in hospital, school or Special Care Unit, there will always be a section in the case notes for medical entries to be recorded. Doctors writing in case notes are laws unto themselves. Admittedly there is a symbolic way for them to write, but this should not be the excuse for illegible scrawl. Someone has to interpret what they say. This task would be made easier if medical staff could be a little more aware of their writing styles. How they wish to write up their own personal notes is entirely up to them, but when it comes to accessible information being available for other disciplines, then there really ought to be a system operational for this to happen.

Of course, there is not a system. What happens is that we all continue to struggle with their hieroglyphics. The longer that this is tolerated, the longer they will continue in this way. But why do we tolerate it? Maybe part of the answer is because we always have. We do not want them to write an idiot's guide to diagnosis, with lengthy explanations. All we want is something that we can read. If within that there are words that we do not understand, we can then refer to the appropriate textbook for our own explanations. We seem to derive sadistic pleasure over the interpretations of what the medics have written. Alongside the medical input, there are other professional fingers in the pie. Psychologists, physiotherapists, speech therapists, and so on, all have something to say in their own jargonised way. Having these reports is important. I am not suggesting that they have no value, or ought to be filed in the waste bin. The information that they convey is crucial to the care plan for the child or adult. At least, it would be crucial if the reports were legible.

Case notes can be compared to jigsaw puzzles. Many disciplines are requested to give their views and opinions. The information collected is put together. This gives part of the picture. This gives the history, with some suggestions of what might be put into action. The hardest part is piecing together the other pieces of the puzzle. It is one thing to ask the various disciplines to contribute their assessments of the child, but it is quite another to present a cohesive and overall picture, with a clear plan for future work. Each discipline will view problems in a different light. They may all suggest ways and means of dealing with them. This is where the multidisciplinary approach really comes into its own. The skill lies in being able to have an overview of the handicapped person. If we are able to see the person as a complete person, not segmented into bits for the various disciplines, then the way will be made clear for a practical assessment procedure to take place. But how best to go about this?

There needs to be a realistic and practical approach to aspects of care. Future planning can never be effective unless the present is clear. The present is dependent on the past. Unfortunately there is a tendency to rely on the past to the point of it interfering with any progress that might be made. Very often, activities that have been tried before and have failed are noted as being failures never to be tried again. They may have been failures in the past, for all sorts of reasons, but this should never be the criterion for not trying them again. Nothing remains static. Things are changing all the time. Maybe the timing was not right when it was tried before.

Maybe the staffing allocation was inappropriate. There are thousands of reasons why things do not work first time round. If we gave up on everything we tried first time round because it did not work, then we would never get anything done. Previous experience must be taken into account, but positively. The past can provide us with a picture of how the person was, which is very relevant to how they are now. We must be objective enough in our work now to be able to look at how the picture has changed from then and try to isolate the reasons as to why this has come about.

My biggest headache has always been trying to find the completed picture from case notes. Nobody has ever condensed the previous information into a shortened form. So that when I am looking through case notes, I have to plough through hundreds of reports written by all sorts of people, in all sorts of ways. All of it very relevant, but time-consuming. For the leader of the Unit/class/ward there is a responsibility for doing summaries. If schools would write more comprehensive reports when the child leaves, instead of forwarding the pile of notes for others to continue to plough through, then this would not only save time, it would also enable everyone to have a much clearer picture of what had been going on. This would lead to a clearer picture of what might happen. It is up to us all to write in clear and legible terms. We are not going to stay with this person for ever. Someone will take over from us one day. Have we so little value of our work that we are unable to convey it to paper? It says nothing to record that Sue likes music. It says a lot if we are told that she likes to listen to classical music and folk songs, but hates pop music. It would also help to know whether she was able to hold an instrument or not. Is it because she can't, or because she won't, or because she doesn't like it?

NEGATIVE REPORTS

Too easily we fall into the trap of negative reporting. Because we have to write something, we resort to writing nothing. For instance, 'Dave has had a quiet day, couldn't get him interested in anything that was going on.' Well maybe this is not his fault. Maybe what we are offering was not to his liking. Why can't we say that we were unadventurous enough in our ideas? Why do we always project the negativity onto handicapped people?

Constant negative reporting will soon lead to negative attitudes. This is so easily conveyed to those who have to follow us. We need to ask ourselves why it is that we prefer the negative qualities. Are they reflective of the negative qualities within ourselves? Maybe part of this process is that we set targets and objectives that are beyond the reach and scope of our groups. We have terrible habits of generalising, and need to be constantly reminded that we are dealing with the individual. Just because the programme for John is working well, it must not lead us to assume that because the same programme is not working for Jane, then it is Jane's fault.

ASSESSING WHAT?

You cannot make an assessment if you are unclear about what it is you are trying to assess. So before you start to work out complicated programmes and planning charts, you need to stand back from the situation so you can gain your sense of direction. Looking at the situation realistically, ask yourself what it is at the end of the day that is important. Is it going to be that Brian will fasten his shoe laces? How long are you going to allow for this to happen? Are you going to try to do anything else at the same time? Are there definite areas of improvement being made using a particular technique? Can you adapt this technique to another situation? What exactly is it that you are trying to achieve? Are these achievements for your benefit, because it is going to enhance your justification for doing this job, or are they in the best interests of the person you are working with?

You have to be honest in your outlook. Wasting time teaching skills that are of no use to the child or adult will not improve their quality of life. Do you want them to be able to hold a cup so that eventually they are going to be able to feed themselves or will you continue to spoon feed them anyway? Are you trying to encourage them to go to the toilet on their own or are you always going to be standing over them in a supervisory capacity?

Ask yourself what it really is that you are setting out to do. Will you get support from others? Are parents going to agree with you? Are they going to reinforce this at home? Will this be an action that is only going to happen in your unit while you are there? When a joint decision has been made about what it is that is going to be the target, then again, realistically and practically, choose the best line of attack. Set simple goals and work out the best way of achieving them.

Brief notes on the breakdown of the activity in question will give you clear and instant feedback on whether you are on the right lines or not. Be generous with your time limits. The profoundly handicapped child has enough restrictions to cope with without having to deal with your neurosis about your time.

It is important that other members of the team are aware of what you are trying to do. The best way of conveying this is to tell them. Failing that, a small card on the office board, or inside the case notes, can give an instant picture to others who are involved in their care. None of us have the time to write copious notes after every session. It is unrealistic to think that we ever will. Brainstorming notes for yourself, and others if they are interested, will suffice. Instigate the discipline to expand on them after a period of six or eight weeks.

All profoundly handicapped children and adults are within a setting that facilitates reviews of their progress. It is important that as many people involved in their care as possible can be present. If this cannot be arranged, insist on something in writing. Any discipline worth their status can never argue with this. It is a responsibility to record work done. Ensure that the future planning made at the review is recorded. Let everyone know what was decided and make sure that all parties are pulling together.

RECORDING

It may be that you are concentrating on vocabulary work. In a session where possibly three or four words are used that you feel need to be recorded, it is inconvenient to jump up and rush to the office for case notes. Try keeping a card index box actually in the work room. This will easily accommodate everybody's progress card, and they are far more accessible than the bulky case notes. If the recording process seems to be more accessible, then it is more likely that it will be used. No one is expecting miracles, but the smallest thing is worth recording, if you feel that it has been progress. A smile, eye contact, response, . . ., all important pieces of the puzzle.

Measurement is something that I find often ignored. When there is such profundity of handicap, it is very hard sometimes to find anything on which to form the base for working. When I was working with Geoffrey, I thought he looked as if he had grown. I measured him and he was 52 inches. He was definitely longer than he was when he had been first admitted, but there was no way of checking this out, as he had never previously been measured. The increased amount of physiotherapy and physical attention that he was having was obviously making some impression on his stretching out capabilities. All those working with him who had visibly seen the difference in his abilities to straighten his legs had no proof that in fact there had been any improvement at all. And all for the sake of noting measurement.

My recommendations as to what to record, chart and monitor are merely those areas that are really important to the welfare of the child or adult. How they are recorded is left to the individual to decide — taking into account the culture and nature of the institution. Keeping it simple is the best advice. Sometimes what we forget is that long after we have gone, someone else in the caring profession will be referring back to our notes. What we write and report is very important to the future for those in our care. We may not envisage leaving the Unit for some years, but nevertheless we must take into account very seriously what it is we are committing to paper. The odd flippant phrase can have damaging results. Case notes can end up in Coroner's Courts. What we say must be responsible and it must, above all else, be honest and objective.

If achievements are not being reached, then we must also be aware of all the possible causes. It is very easy to put the blame on the handicapped person. Is that the only way to look at it? Who is to blame? Is it the programme? Is it the parents? Is it the system? Is it us?

Case notes are for a lifetime. Their contents reflect the opinions and the attitudes of staff. They ought to reflect the current position of the child or adult, with ideas as to how their lifestyle and quality of life can be improved. As contributors to this, are we ever really doing enough?

The Best Place to Be

MOVING OUT

Integration is a word frequently used. As the plans to close down more wards become operational, small but increasing numbers of patients are leaving hospitals to take up their lives in the community. The long-term planning envisages community life for all.

I would never argue the case for integration not taking place. I feel that, for many handicapped people, a move to the community will provide a more stimulating and valuable lifestyle than that provided by the institution. But to move out involves careful planning, careful teaching and careful preparation for those embarking on the new life 'out there'. But these same aspects need as much if not more investment for people already living in the community. The community isn't ready for a mass exodus of residents from hospital. The community has not got the resources to cope with the numbers and it is not yet ready or prepared to share the problems that are inevitably going to arise. So while on the one hand we may be striving hard to improve skills and independence, on the other we are often prevented from seeing an end product taking shape.

For the profoundly handicapped children and adults who need constant care and physical attention, are they going to be able to find their place in the community? Can this group really be integrated? Whatever we may feel about moving out, the practicalities of it will ultimately be dealt with on a political and economic level. How we manage what we are doing between now and then could very well influence what will eventually happen — and more importantly, how it will happen. We must have a clear sense of direction. We need to be looking not just at what we are doing today, but at how it relates to tomorrow.

If we are not careful then the tomorrows will quickly pass us by and, before we know where we are, changes will be made without our views being known. The difficulties arise when we become so involved with the immediate problems: low staffing levels, lack of resources, the demands of those we care for and so on. It is so easy to take each day as it comes — resolving the here-and-now problems as the priorities. The amount of energy that this takes often drains the energy still needed to look at tomorrow. But until we can find time and space to plan long term, with clearly defined goals and objectives that are in context with the entirety of the situation, then the value of the work being done today will lose it's worth.

STAYING PUT

A great number of profoundly handicapped people will inevitably never be able to leave the residential care setting that they are now in. For families who care for their son or daughter at home now, the realities of the situation are that they will not be able to continue to provide this care for ever. Despite the current trends to move out, resources to build new units and hostels are very limited and so, looking at the problem from a purely practical and economic viewpoint, institutions will be with us for a considerable time to come.

For those practitioners working in residential settings, they will see a lot of activity in the community, but could well be in positions of not being part of it. For those staff and their residents, together they will be the groups who stay put. They may see themselves as being the 'ones who got left behind'.

For all the positive reasoning that can be presented for staying put, there are a number of negative responses that will inevitably arise. If money is being invested into community hostels and units, there will be little left over for hospitals. Staff may see this as a reinforcing factor for their low esteem. It must be difficult not to get upset over being left behind. From the residents' viewpoint, there are advantages to staying. The routine will not be disrupted, the surroundings will not change, faces will stay familiar, and so on. From the staff viewpoint it is very different. The work is as demanding — and suddenly nobody seems to find that it is worth any more investment. To find ourselves in the left-behind group, we must remember that we are not being forgotten. We have a very valuable role to play.

The security that is afforded the institution is a great comfort to those in our care. Consistency and continuity of care is very important to handicapped people. If we feel threatened by what's going on 'out there', our anxiety levels will increase and will hinder the quality of care we are offering. Wherever we are — in or out — our main objectives should be the same.

Mismanagement

TO TELL OR NOT TO TELL

The reasons why incidents or mismanagement occur are as diverse as the reasons why they do not. As practitioners in this field, as in any other within the caring professions, we ought to be striving towards improving quality of care.

Opportunities for further, and even different, training are more available in the 1980s than they were ten, twenty or thirty years ago. The population generally tends to move around with more frequency, and so now there is not so much 'stagnation in post' occurring. Other disciplines have established their roles in the institution, so that what was once seen as being primarily a very closed and predominantly nursing area is now a far more open, varied and multidisciplinary environment.

All this — and a lot more — has gone a long way towards dispelling some of the myths surrounding mental handicap. As special schools operate integration policies and move their children out into community state schools, then this too has helped open up the area of mental handicap even further. The media have brought our attention to incidents of mismanagement and over recent years there have been new policies and procedures in operation to protect further the interests and welfare of mentally handicapped people. But old habits die hard and there are still incidents of mismanagement occurring even now, despite the progress and changes that have been made.

As I see it, there are principally three main problem areas:

(i) Establishing the reasons why mismanagement occurs.
(ii) Establishing ways of preventing mismanagement from occurring.
(iii) Deciding what we are going to do about it.

Without delving too deeply I would just like to mention very briefly some of my own feelings.

There seems to be very clear patterns of copying behaviour in almost any profession. As learners, we tend to adopt those patterns set us by our seniors. If we are shown or told that a way of doing something is the right way, or the only way, then without any experience or knowledge to draw upon, we often believe that what has been shown to us is in fact the right way. But what if it isn't the right way? What if it is done in this way to save time and cut corners? What if it is done this way to suit staff and not to suit the people we are caring for? What if we feel that it isn't right? Can we say so? Do we say so? What happens to us? What happens to those in our care?

There is so much energy and excitement being generated within the field of profound handicap at the moment that it would be taking a very negative attitude to dwell unnecessarily on any of these issues. The subject is a very emotive one but mention does need to be made nonetheless — but where to start? I suppose the only place we can start is with ourselves. Standards of care are under discussion here. We provide the standards, so any drop in those standards has to be directly attributable to the practitioners — be they staff, parents or guardians. Asking ourselves why is a very good base on which we can start.

Why do we feed John in that way?
Why do we put Sarah in that position?

Why do we talk about Sam as if he isn't there?
Why does Colin have to get up at six o'clock?
Why can't Mollie sit in a chair so that she can see what is going on?
Why? Why? Why? If the question is asked enough times, then the right answers will eventually be found. It is when there are no reasonable answers that it is really time to question why in a major way. There should never be a day go by without us having to ask why.

Support Systems

COUNSELLING

Earlier in the book there is reference made to the lack of counselling that was available to parents. Here I would like to spend some time discussing the part that we can all play in this very important service.

Counselling in the professional sense takes years of training. Some professionals undertake the training and some do not. But as practitioners and parents working in the field of profound handicap, we all at some time or another need to have counselling ourselves, or are in positions whereby we are needed to provide counselling for others. For the purposes of this book, I would like to offer as my reference point the following definition:

Counselling is facilitating time to listen to what is being said and giving clarity to what is being presented as a difficulty.

There are many situations and circumstances whereby parents or families want to unload a particular problem that they are experiencing, but feel unable or unwilling to turn to others for help. If they have only experienced counselling in an emergency situation, then they may feel that they can only have this service if in fact there is an emergency. The general day-to-day problems of running a home and family and career are reasons enough for needing a sympathetic ear from time to time. But caring for a profoundly handicapped child or adult simply doubles the pressures that parents have to cope with every day.

I find it sad when parents make comments like, 'I'm so very lucky that Julie can come here each day. If it all stopped tomorrow I'd still feel grateful for what she has had.' When assured that this has not got anything to do with luck, that this is a right, Julie's mother is insistent, almost as if she doesn't deserve to have the support.

Families that are able to share the handicap are lucky, but unfortunately these families are few and far between. Inevitably one parent will take on more than the other, and once the pattern is established it then becomes very difficult to break. Taking over more of the physical side of the caring will ultimately lead to taking on more of the psychological problems. If the other partner is reluctant or refuses to share the work, then there is a build-up of emotion and conflict, tolerated only to a certain degree before it finds its outlet.

One-parent families, trying to be all things to all people, are often psychologically much better off than these two-parent family units. At least they know that there isn't going to be another partner coming home at five o'clock for tea. I sometimes wonder which is worse — having someone around who takes no interest, or not having anyone around at all? Parents can't switch off from their handicapped son or daughter. Without regular support there are no formal channels for this energy to be directed and the parent then has to swallow hard and take on more and more. The silliest, slightest difficulties then grow out of all proportion until explosion point is reached. Counselling in an intervention sense is then available — but only because there is a crisis.

In the plans for moves into the community, and the plans for enabling as many profoundly handicapped youngsters as is possible to live at home, counselling must be given priority consideration. It is totally unreasonable to ask and expect parents to cope with all they have to cope with without giving them the support that they need to fulfil their roles adequately.

Support and counselling are not commodities that should only be given in times of crisis. By creating regular opportunities for meeting with and talking to parents, the practitioners can establish good trusting relationships and form the links that need to be made. In the event that an emergency does arise, the parents will at least know who they are talking to and not have to explain a complicated history to a stranger every time they pick up the phone and shout for help. It must be said that there are a great many families who manage very well without a support service. Maybe this is because their very own support systems from friends work very well. But there are even greater numbers who manage well because they have always had to manage well and have never known things to be any different. From the birth of the baby or on-set of the handicap, counselling should be available and it should be consistent and regular. A quick phone call once a year is an insult.

Parents need to relocate their value and sense of worth and purpose. These are all areas that they lose and are often un-able to find again on their own. As practitioners, can we really honestly say that helping these parents to help their children is 'not our job'? If parents know that there is someone, somewhere who knows of and understands their family, and that person can be contacted, this is very often all that is needed if they are having a bad day. Knowing that it can be talked about the next day or the next week is enough to keep them going and prevent something untoward from happening.

From the very beginning good support services must be established. Families are never constant and there are periods of time when everything seems to be going well and then black patches that make the future full of despair. Parents need to be reminded of the good times, so that they can be helped to draw upon their own resources in ways that can help them to overcome the bad times. All the counselling in the world is not going to take the handicap away — we know that. But by giving support we can help those who have to care to be able to care for much longer.

WHO NEEDS FRIENDS?

Vanessa and Martin, teaching colleagues and friends of mine, were very excited about the long-awaited baby Vanessa was carrying. At twenty weeks, following a scan, they were told that the 'baby was not developing normally' and arrangements were made for admission the following day for a termination of pregnancy. The following week they went to stay with her family for the remainder of the school holidays. Back at work and still reeling from the shock of what had happened, they both discovered that their friends had formed themselves into two very separate groups. Quite a number phoned regularly with offers of tea and sympathy and invitations to 'talk about it'. But there were also quite a few who could not cope with the situation at all.

I should now like to take up some issues regarding this latter group. Friends knew that a welcomed expectant baby had been lost. They knew that it was the first baby and they knew that Vanessa was in her mid-thirties. Having all these facts at hand though, they made frequent comments such as:

'Don't worry, have another one.'

'There's plenty of time, it can't happen again.'

'It's just one of those things.'

'What bad luck, how's the badminton going?'

'Did you have a nice holiday?'

Apart from the things that were said, their subsequent approach and behaviour towards the couple changed quite remarkably. On the occasions when they did meet, they looked embarrassed, almost as if they were somehow trying to compensate for the tragedy, or were boisterous and over-jolly, cracking jokes and making light of everything.

Some friends never got the opportunity to behave in this way, as they cleverly managed to engineer circumstances so that any confrontation just never took place. People sent letters of condolence, expressing their sorrow, but when meeting the couple these same people pretended that nothing at all had been acknowledged, and simply asked if the holiday had been a success. No reference at all was made to the tragedy. In fact no reference was made to them even writing about it. This group could easily convey their thoughts and feelings on paper, but were unable to acknowledge the same feelings when in the company of the very people they were supposedly trying to console.

Vanessa very much needed some space to be able to talk about what had happened. There was little that anyone would do or say that was going to change the circumstances. What had happened had happened. But what she did find of comfort was the opportunity to verbalise how she felt — being able to talk about it was a relief to the tension that she was bottling up inside. Knowing that everyone knew what had happened, when confronted by someone who refused even to acknowledge it, she became defensive and awkward, and, to be able to cope at all, turned the feelings in on herself, where they built up to explosion point.

All she really wanted was the acknowledgement that the person talking to her knew. A simple 'I'm so sorry, if there's anything I can do . . .', would have been enough. To have had this acknowledgement would have relieved the anxiety, and enabled normal conversation to follow and the tension to dissipate. But not having the acknowledgement, and seeing the embarrassment and listening to the strained conversation, only reinforced her own embarrassment. She told me that there were days when she started to wonder if in fact any of her trauma had actually happened at all. When surrounded by people who completely blotted out that awful week in her life, she too began to think that maybe it had been just a terrible nightmare after all.

The transfer of embarrassment happened so quickly. Almost instantly she picked up these feelings, and started to collude with them. These friends could not handle their own feelings and as their defences could not allow any conversation about the termination to take place, they projected this on to Vanessa. What they were in fact telling her was:

'I'm terrified, it could happen to me.'

'Don't talk to me about it, then I won't have to talk to you about it.'

To be able to deal with Vanessa and Martin at all, they felt they had to carry on as if nothing had happened at all. By removing this week from all their lives, then there was no reason to talk about it. Without the tragedy, then relationships could stay as they were and conversations could be conducted as they were. Vanessa and Martin were put into situations whereby certain behaviour and conversation was expected of them. As the expectations were so forcefully placed upon them, they found themselves not only colluding with these feelings, but matching themselves up to what friends needed them to be.

Vanessa needed the space to be as she was — not to be how others wanted her to be. But she soon began to smile readily and tell people that she felt fine, when this was very far from the truth. But this was just what everyone wanted. Things had to be fine so everyone could cope. Everyone except Vanessa and Martin that is. But things weren't fine. The pregnancy, or mini-pregnancy, had changed so much. Vanessa described how the baby had done incredible things to her body and her mind. And then quite suddenly just as these changes were beginning to be accepted, the pregnancy was over. The anticlimax of having to go through the stages of labour, knowing that there was going to be nothing at the end of it, except the finality of it all and the despair.

During the mourning of the loss, as with all mourning, there must be time and space for those who are bereaved to be able to mourn. It was no consolation to Vanessa and Martin to know that they could have another baby. They needed to be able to come to terms with losing their first.

One of the ways that this process could have been helped could have come from friends — friends who were willing to put 'friendship' before their own feelings. Friends who could say that it was OK to cry. Friends who could have provided a shoulder to cry on. Vanessa and Martin, and other couples in similar circumstances, need the contact and support. They never expected anyone to make everything right by simply saying or doing the right thing at the right time. They merely needed people around to share some of their feelings, thereby sharing their sorrow, and thereby relieving some of the anxiety and stress. What they did not need was to have friends provoking the anxiety by their own embarrassment.

In situations like this, counselling is imperative to both partners — both individually and together. Martin's main concern lay with Vanessa's well-being. But he needed to have the support to enable him to support his wife. In groups of family or friends, so many people ignored Vanessa and then asked Martin why she was being so quiet. Almost as if they were blind to her even being there.

Tragedy of any description cannot be ignored. Yes, things need to get back to normal as soon as possible, but subsequent normality will never be the same following trauma. Support has to be given so that the people being counselled can find the resources within themselves to establish a new normality. The deliberate withdrawal of support, or the inability to acknowledge that it is even needed, will only add to the pain and reinforce it further.

The social networks surrounding the family with a handicapped child or adult play a very important role to those families. Parents don't need to feel handicapped themselves. They need support to be able to come to terms with the drastic changes in their lives. This is not something that is needed now and again, it is needed all the time. They feel ill at ease enough about taking their handicapped son or daughter out for tea, or inviting friends round for a chat. But if they can see that their friends want their company, for no other reason than wanting their company, then that in itself is supportive and comforting. Being embarrassed and awkward, conducting strained conversation or not knowing what to talk about only makes circumstances so much worse than they already are.

Unable to deal with this strain often leads to loss of contact — because both friends and parents find the whole thing far too anxiety-provoking. This adds to the isolation that handicapped families suffer far too frequently, and turning the feelings in on themselves, they end up believing not only that their child is not wanted but that they too are not wanted. If only friends could overcome these defensive ways and see their friends for what they are, acknowledging the handicap and all it entails, then parents will find that they can relax, and truly appreciate the value of being accepted in a normal way. This will lead to normal conversation, normal activity, normal socialisation. Yes, there will be problems. Yes, it won't be easy in the initial stages. But surely these parents have to be given the opportunities to be able to experience some sense of normality?

GAINING CONFIDENCE

Parents who take more and more on board are often so totally committed and involved in the well-being of their son or daughter that they are unable to see what is actually happening to the overall situation. When behavioural problems get out of hand, and nothing seems to work to relieve the situation, many parents feel inadequate and incompetent. As confidence levels drop, they often find that they can't do anything right. Day-to-day chores that they once dealt with very competently suddenly become huge insurmountable problems. With anxiety levels on the increase, the situation soon gets out of control. But with regular support, it will be easier for the counsellor to see these patterns emerging, and be instrumental in drawing attention to them. If alternatives can be found in the early stages, then problems that may have followed can be prevented from happening.

It must be remembered that the problems and difficulties that can present themselves in one month, or one year, are rarely going to be the same as those presented at another time. Of course there are recurring problems, but moods and circumstances are always changing. As people get older, experiences and energy levels differ and incentive and motivation alters. To keep on top of all these inner changes, an outside factor needs to be constant. This need can best be met by counselling. As the services offered to profoundly handicapped people and their families vary so much, there are no standard or formalised guidelines to draw upon.

Working within the restraints of localised budgets and resources, it becomes an impossible task to decide who will provide counselling, and for whom. Ideally those people specifically trained to counsel will provide the most effective service. But all practitioners involved must take on board some of the responsibility for ensuring not only that it does actually happen for families but that it also happens for themselves.

4   Halfway There:
A Conclusion so Far

As it was difficult to make a start on this book, so now it is equally difficult to conclude the first part. By looking at some of the issues that affect our functioning as practitioners, and people, and by discussing some issues that affect profoundly handicapped people themselves, I have tried to get in touch with some of the feelings involved. We will be ineffective in our work if we ignore what is going on within ourselves. But having insight into how we feel will make our work much easier — not physically, but psychologically. If we can be at peace, then this is something that we can easily transfer to those in our care.

It is not enough to have a 'handbook' of ideas and, armed with this, have some sort of guarantee that what you use from it will work. Getting equipment does not mean getting results. You have to start much nearer to home, with yourself. Honesty is the best policy, and if you haven't got what it takes, then it is much better to leave well alone. If you have a belief that something can be done, and a realistic attitude towards your own resources, then you are well on the way to making a start.

What is needed in this field of work is something that goes beyond being a 'minder'. Given the right circumstances, we can all bring ourselves to care for someone's basic needs, but the severely handicapped child needs much more than just basic care. We have to get beyond the casing that is their body, and somehow reach to their mind. In providing a better quality of life, we have truly to *believe* that they have the capacity to learn — our role is to find ways of bringing that learning about. This demands of us certain attitudes. We cannot presume that what will work for one will automatically work for another. We have to find the one individual key that will open the door for progress to be made. Once we have found the key, then the ideas and suggestions are useful. The problem is finding the key.

Because we are all human, it goes without saying that we cannot expect to get on with everyone all the time. We all have preferences in who we hit it off with, and the same can be said of those in our care. If personality clashes are a problem, it is not the end of the world. If we try to work through the dislike, we are making the situation much worse than it already is. It may be that we feel very uncomfortable with some people. In my experience, I have always found that where there are personality clashes, another member of staff has felt the exact opposite. It is always better to start off on the right foot, and if the shoes don't fit, then don't wear them. And more importantly, don't make anyone else wear them either. Initial gut reactions often are right. You are doing yourself and those in your care a great disservice if you ignore these signals.

We have to ask ourselves if our flexibility will be beneficial or not. If we are used to working in a highly structured way, following particular schools of thought, is this going to get results? Well, there are more ways than one of looking at this problem. Routine is necessary. It provides boundaries, and creates a sense of consistency, which are needed when working with handicapped people. The dangers are that it can also provide an institutionalised environment. What is needed is a happy and comfortable compromise. Routine yes, but with built-in flexibility for changes, as and when necessary.

Having decided on a definite plan of action, are you able to change this at a minute's notice? Can you take up the feel of the mood of the group and work with this, despite previously deciding on something quite different? Are you able to start where the handicapped person is at, rather than where you are at? If the answer to these questions is 'no', then what follows will be of little use to you.

And Now to Work

5 Building Relationships

Learning will not take place until a relationship has been established. We all interpret levels of relationships in different ways, so I do not want to spend time discussing 'types of relationship'. My own feeling is that there comes a time when 'something' happens, and instinctively you know that you have a basis on which you can build. For some, this 'time' may take months to present itself — for others, it happens very quickly. The danger is to lose heart if the process is not happening as fast as you may want it to. When this happens, you still 'go through the motions' but not with the same interest and enthusiasm, and this is quickly picked up by the handicapped person and can have very negative repercussions. Allowances must be made for off-days by both parties. There is no specific time limit set on objectives like these being reached. If it is taking longer than anticipated, go along with it — it *will* happen sooner or later.

Observation

I always find it useful to observe from a distance. I look for movement, eye contact, mannerisms, interaction with others. This not only gives me some 'instant' information but also allows me time to 'take in' appearance. While observing, I can also start thinking about various activities that may be useful. When watching someone in a group, there is also the opportunity to see if any of the group dynamics are affected by the new group member. If attention is given, does this spark off attention-seeking behaviour by one of the others? It is also of interest to notice if the attitudes of the staff are also affected

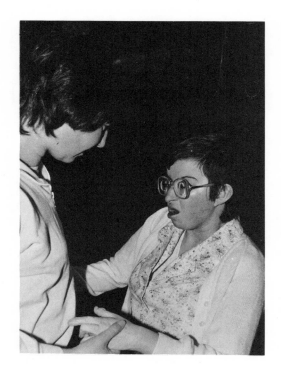

by the new group member. This 'observation' time gives me some space to formulate ideas and allows the opportunity to collect any pieces of equipment that I might need to have before starting work, such as tissues.

The Approach

However your group or individual is positioned, then that's where you start, and always on their level, not yours. It is very intimidating to stand over someone. The floor is very safe, and I always prefer to have the first introduction there. If the person is able to sit up, or if they have no support and are lying down, then I tend to adopt the same posture. Softly saying their name and introducing yourself is very important.

Case Study

During a dramatherapy workshop for nurses working in a residential setting, we were exploring some of the issues concerned with communication. I asked the group to sit on the floor with their respective partners for one of the exercises. Although everyone involved themselves in what followed, it was obvious that there were some participants who found this exercise particularly difficult. Later in discussion, it transpired that for many of the group, 'working on the floor' was the aspect that had caused the conflict.

'It's not *what* we were doing on the floor that bothered me', said one, 'It was the fact that I just don't like being on the floor. I don't think the floor is a socially acceptable place to be. I spend all day asking residents to get off the floor and sit on chairs, and now you're asking me to do the reverse. I'm sorry, but I don't think residents should be encouraged to sit on the floor.'

As with so many other issues, the practitioner must decide 'what's best'. I have my own views on this one, as you must have yours. My inclusion of the conversation is to remind you of two very important points:

1. There will always be another way of looking at any issue.
2. There is always a reason as to *why* this should be so.

The severity of the handicap should never deter you from using normal social graces. If the person is aphasic, and grossly physically handicapped, this does not give us the right to presume that there is no comprehension of the spoken word. It is extremely rude to conduct a conversation about somebody in their presence, as if they were not there, and this applies to handicapped people as much as it would were they non-handicapped. Unfortunately, this is something that happens a lot: the assumption that profound disability makes a person both deaf and lacking in emotional depth. We have no way of knowing that this is so.

When communication is one-way only, that is from practitioner to handicapped person, we can use the tone of our voice to convey reassurance. It really does not matter what the topic of conversation is — the weather, how they are, and so on. If the tone used is calm and gentle, then this will go a long way towards lowering anxiety levels that may have risen due to the newness of the situation and the worker.

Getting Close

The next step is to make physical contact. Holding hands, and stroking, are both non-threatening and soothing. Depending on the reaction, you can then decide on what to do next. If the person is lying down, then lie down with them. Try and maintain eye contact, keeping the conversation going, but softly. This should be done for at least fifteen minutes.

What you are doing is allocating time for this person only and no one else. It is no good simply to say a few words and then go away, and come back half an hour later and repeat the exercise. You have to let the person see that you are willing to spend some time with them. They have to know that they have your attention for more than just a few minutes, and to the exclusion of everyone else.

During this time, although concentration spans may be poor, you are enabling them to have a 'closer' look at you. It might take months before they can give you any sign of recognition, but you have to allow for lack of concentration,

and also for enough time for your voice and your face to become familiar. They have no way of knowing whether you are going to be someone who will be a regular feature in their lives or whether you are just 'passing through'. They need lots of time to work all this out.

In these first stages, you may be on the receiving end of a certain amount of 'testing'. It might not suit them to have someone pay them so much attention as they may not be used to it. Because this is a new experience, and one that has not had to be dealt with previously, one way of dealing with it is to try and stop it, by sending you away.

Case Study

Polly was twenty-four, heart complaint, epileptic and immobile. She had spent most of her time in the Unit on her own, in a corner, as she had quite violent tendencies. This gave her tremendous power. Every time she did not want to do something, she threw something or bit someone, and this was instantly followed by her being isolated. She could virtually do as she pleased. It was decided that she would join in the physical activities in the morning, which was clearly something she was very opposed to doing. As an effort to get out of it, she systematically ripped the collars off everyone's Tee-shirts. This caused disruption to the activity — which was exactly what she wanted. It worked to a degree. There was a split in staff. Some decided that it was not worth more Tee-shirts, others just wore old Tee-shirts when working with Polly.

It did not take long for Polly to get the message. We did not care about the Tee-shirts, we cared about her non-involvement. She is now fully involved in the Unit activities, but it did not come about overnight. Once we had managed to include her in one activity, which she clearly enjoyed, it then did not take too long to start introducing her gradually to others. The whole process took about eighteen months.

She put us all to the test, and it paid off. It would have been far easier to have played it her way and there were times when we came near to defeat. But to see her now, participating fully, was well worth all the ripped Tee-shirts.

Doing Nothing

In the early stages, when it is difficult to decide just what you are going to do, there is always the option of not doing anything. By just being with someone is of value. Because you are a professional does not mean that you have to be forever 'doing' something. Getting to know someone takes time, on both sides. And you can't always hurry the process along. You can hold them, sit with them and lie down with them. You do not have to have any equipment. You yourself can be enough.

Allowing yourself to be 'close' physically is very important. By reducing distance, you are enhancing the relationship. If this person can feel that you *want* to be close, they will allow this to happen, and that closeness can be another brick with which to start building the relationship.

6   Being Practical

Using Sounds

Sounds can be a very useful medium. They can be used in a variety of ways and with all types of groups. As with many activities used when working with handicapped people, sounds can be instrumental in widening horizons, creating a stimulating environment, encouraging expression and, of course, making work 'fun'. For the person who does not speak, for whatever reason, sounds may be the mechanism that can be employed to prompt response. As discussed earlier, 'the spoken word' as we know it is not the be all and end all of communication. We must be forever on the look-out for methods that can improve communication channels.

There are lots of lovely sounds that can be made without the use of tape recorders and expensive equipment.

Case Study

Diane, aged twenty-nine, would speak very occasionally, and never more than two or three words at a time; for example, 'Good morning', 'Steady now', 'Gently'. Her spoken vocabulary was limited, although it was felt that she had quite a good comprehension of what was said to her. We had started to play some vocabulary games, but the responses were very erratic. One day she would capably anticipate the words, and then the next not be able to say any of them.

But in one of her sessions I heard her say 'swish'. Her diction was clear, and she kept repeating it, and was obviously enjoying the 'game'. When I started saying 'swish', she squealed with delight. We varied this and used 'swash', 'swush', 'sweesh', 'swoooosh'. It was definitely the 'sh' sound that was giving the pleasure. The next session we continued with vocabulary games, but instead of using 'swish', etc., we started on 'push', with the action, gently pushing her back, then encouraging her to do the same with me, always saying the word each time. This led to 'wash' (with action) and 'bash' (gently!), always with the emphasis on the 'sh' sound. The actions were always two-way, and soon Diane started to say the correct word for the appropriate action.

The success of building in yet one more word into a working vocabulary did not come overnight. As with many activities, it is difficult to measure the success by virtue of the fact that many severely handicapped people are unable to have the opportunity of using the new word in different circumstances, away from the practitioner.

Some six months later, Diane was 'waddling' by me on her way to the toilet block. She placed one hand in the middle of my back and gave an almighty shove, as she shouted 'push'. It was only then that we realised that the word had been built in and could be used in separate circumstances from the learning situation.

Case Study

Steven, aged twenty, had no vocabulary, but was able to make sounds. We soon realised that sounds were more forthcoming when he had something to hold. He would turn his head towards the object and make an 'aaaa' sound, and then smile.

By introducing short words, with objects each time, we soon began to increase his sound vocabulary. 'Ooooo' and 'Eeeee' were the first improvements, followed by the introduction of an extra letter, as in 'Pow', 'Now', 'Boo', 'Bee' and so on.

It is almost impossible to establish the extent of how much progress has been made, in terms of comprehension of vocabulary, but what has been achieved is a workable usage of different sounds. They may not be all that communicative in themselves, but they have been stimulating in that they have brought great pleasure to Steven and to those working with him — not least, of course, his family.

Case Study

> Charlie, aged twenty, a member of a Special Needs Group, seemed to have a reasonable comprehension of the spoken word, but was unable to communicate in English, although he did have quite a large vocabulary of gobbledegook. Listening intently to what he actually said, and then trying to repeat it, resulted in him getting very excited. After two or three sessions, using *his* language, we soon extended *our* vocabulary.

At first it was strange using new words, but for Charlie, the anxiety levels were much lowered. He knew what we were talking about, and tried very hard to help us to learn new words. By opening up the communication channels, he became more involved with the activities, and the tendency to take himself off into a corner became an infrequent occurrence.

USING TAPE RECORDERS

I have used cassette recorders with many different groups and found them to be an important piece of equipment. With a Special Needs Group, where language was a major area of concern, we taped the sessions so we could play back the tapes later for reference and analysis. Having the equipment in the room did not seem to be a distracting element for the group. Without any prompting from staff, group members would clear the table in preparation and took more than a keen interest in the machine. People who refused to join in activities slowly started to involve themselves with the mechanics of taping — squealing with delight at discovering the buttons and volume switches.

Although we had decided to tape the sessions for a limited trial period, we found ourselves in the position of having to continue, as taping became so important to the group. Having got their attention, we played back their sounds, and tried to identify 'who's that?'. This proved to be more successful than we had anticipated. For those in the group who normally were reluctant to make any sounds at all, this was actively encouraging sounds, many that we had not heard previously.

There was great competitive spirit amongst the group. Who could shout the loudest? Who could sing the longest? When we compared our notes from the sessions where we had not used the tapes to those when we had there was a definite improvement in incidence of speech being used.

Following on from this, we decided to continue with vocabulary building and selected sounds which we then taped for use in the session. There are a number of LPs and cassettes on the market which have a variety of sounds, but my favourite is 'Essential Sounds And Effects' (BBC Records). It is a double album and reasonably priced. It has almost every sound effect that you could choose to use. Each section only lasts a few seconds, so I took the sections we were most interested in, and taped them two or three times so that the sections were longer. This helps with groups where concentration spans are short. The first group of sounds we used were animal sounds: dogs, cats, cows, horses, elephants, seals, monkeys, and so on.

The initial reaction was very positive from most members of the group. Those who could speak spontaneously shouted out the name of the animal. Those who could not speak made every effort to use mime to show us that they knew what each animal was. We tried every sound possible, and the sounds that produced the best responses were inevitably the sounds that we had thought were obscure. Likewise, the sounds that we were convinced would stimulate the group nearly always fell flat.

Never underestimate the spontaneity and creativity of the group. Despite carefully laid out plans of action, you must always be aware of the possibilities of having to change the session, and take up the suggestions that come from the group themselves. This is always the best way to work in this sort of situation. Using their ideas gives them so much more confidence, and is far more stimulating than 'forcing' your ideas upon them.

FLEXIBILITY

Be adventurous with sounds chosen, and always remember that you cannot predict what the response is going to be.

Have an open mind, and retain the flexibility to channel their ideas, taking priority over your own. There is great value from using sound work in a group setting, but this is also something that can be used on a one-to-one basis. There are a number of light headphones that can be bought for a few pounds, which enable just one person to use the machine, while other activities are going on.

Linking the sounds of everyday actions can be an important tool that can be used in vocabulary work, as in hand clapping. This is encouraging eye–hand coordination. It is also an action that many severely handicapped people do involuntarily. Taping their own sounds and then playing them back can reinforce the action with the word. There are so many sounds that can be taped this way. A few examples are:

Tapping (objects — table, each other, windows).

Tapping — using an object like a ruler or pencil.

Listening for the different sounds that each object tapped makes.

Crumpling paper (different types of paper make different sounds). Try crumpling cardboard and contrast with tissue paper.

Try tearing paper, and rustling paper, pages in a book, pages in magazines.

Water pouring, splashing, dripping, running, etc.

Again it is important to try to take the ideas of the group rather than impose your own. As with all activities, make sure that your instructions are clear and vocabulary used is concise and not confusing. One of the key aims of sound work is to improve vocabulary, so keep this uppermost in your mind, and use words that are accessible.

Smells and Smells

The smells of incontinence and disinfectants are far more obvious in Special Care Units than whiffs of Christian Dior. Standard-issue talc and soaps could hardly be classified as pampering items. Health and Education Authorities are unlikely to change their budgets to accommodate more expensive and better-quality items, so the responsibility for providing some pampering lies with families and staff.

We must try to be aware of our own standards for personal hygiene and endeavour not to make differences for our handicapped groups.

To start at the top . . . .

HAIR

Standard-issue shampoo allows no room for thought with regard to hair types. It seems quite absurd to believe that the thousands of residents in institutional settings all have the same type of hair and therefore all need the same type of shampoo. Yet there is little provision made to accommodate the differences that occur. Would we wash our hair with shampoo designed for dry hair if our hair was greasy? Of course we wouldn't. If our hair needed conditioner, then we would use it. Why then can't we use it for handicapped people too?

In fact, if we were honest about it, we do very little to assist the appearance of handicapped people in our care. We can all easily think about the reasons why we don't rate this area high on our priority lists, but are our reasons justifiable? I would argue that they are not. Any old trim will *not* do. It wouldn't 'do' for us so why should it 'do' for anybody else?

SOAP

We are fortunate that we have a choice. There are a vast number of soaps on the market from which we can choose, within our budgets, but more importantly to suit ourselves and our skin types. Are we as considerate for those in our care?

BATH TIME

Having a bath should be a pleasurable activity, but unfortunately it can be anxiety-provoking for profoundly handicapped people. The pressure of time, difficulties with dressing and lifting can all be easily transferred from the staff to the individual concerned.

If we are trying to provide a stimulating environment then we cannot afford to let opportunities slip by. There are a range of products available for use in the bath that have very distinctive smells. Raspberry, cucumber, peach, apricot, apple, strawberry and so on are just a few of the bath salts that can be bought at a reasonable price. The smells of these salts are beautiful, they are educational, and they are also fun.

TALCUM POWDER

Most talcum powder has a nice smell about it, and so it really is just a question of whether it is preferred or not. But it should be the preference of the handicapped person and not the staff. Rubbing it into and under folds of flesh is not going to give comfort — it is going to cause distress later on. Where's the sense in applying talc to areas of the body that we know will soon be wet — either through perspiration or incontinence?

SCENT AND AFTERSHAVE

Again, this is a personal view, but I don't think that we use these two items enough. Surely the smell of incontinence cannot be preferred to the smell of good aftershave or good scent? When it is time for giving presents, such as birthdays or Christmas, thought should be given to these things. I cannot argue about finances as each family's and each child's needs are so very diverse. But there must be the opportunity for buying 'the luxuries' of life. Our handicapped people are deprived of so many things that the non-handicapped sector of the community take so much for granted. Yet this is an area that we can do something about.

If finances do not allow the purchasing of what some might call 'extras' (although I do not regard scent and aftershave as extras, I think they are necessities), then a jumble sale or other fund-raising activities could be organised to raise the money to buy them. Items such as these should never be out of reach for handicapped people.

HAND CREAM AND BODY LOTION

If a handicapped person is unable to rub cream into their own hands, then this should not be the criterion employed for not using it. We can rub it in can't we? It can be used as a game. 'Now you see it — now you don't.' There's something very soothing about massaging cream into hands and feet. On the occasions when you are stuck for something to do, this is an excellent activity that can last for as long or as short as you wish. The benefit is twofold. First, you are giving one-to-one attention, and secondly, not only is it pleasurable but it is also stimulating. Try it!

FEET

Feet tend to be ignored. Because they are never used, in terms of standing on, this does not give us the right to pay little attention to them. Feet can become really smelly, and what we as practitioners must do is find a way of preventing this from happening. Soap and water might be all that's needed.

GETTING DOWN TO BASICS

The whole point of including a section on personal hygiene is to remind the reader of the importance of dignity and basic care. When making cases for extra staff, we must put forward the elements of our work that demand our time to be stretched. It is insane to have priorities torn. It isn't a question of whether painting is more important than twenty-five minutes in the bath. They are both important. Neither one should have to suffer at the expense of the other — but they do.

Lipstick stops dribbling. Painted nails look nice. Clean shining hair is appealing. We are supposedly striving for providing a better quality of life. What better place to start than with the body? We know ourselves how much better we feel for having a long soak, or a shower, at the end of the day. We know how refreshing it feels to smell nice. Is it really too much to ask for us to apply the standards that we set ourselves to those we care for?

It's Tasty!

In the search for sensory stimulation activities, the practitioner does not have to look very far beyond the kitchen cupboard. There are literally hundreds of foods that can be listed to facilitate reaction and response. It must be stated that because there may not be any visible response this should never be the criterion used for not even trying.

Taking into careful consideration any dietary or feeding complications, activities used for taste can also incorporate vocabulary and signing work. Added to this of course is the pure enjoyment of being able to eat or drink something at a time other than a designated eating or drinking time.

ONE LUMP OR TWO?

I wish to make use of this section to discuss how one particular feeding method, used frequently with profoundly handicapped people, is undertaken with less than their best interests at heart. Yes, you've guessed it — the liquidiser!

Entire meals are tipped in, the machine is switched on and hey presto!, instant liquidised revolting looking unidentifiable pulp is ready to be served. What a shame that each separate component of the meal cannot be tasted. Is it really so much trouble to liquidise meat and vegetables separately? By churning everything up together, we are making no allowances for establishing if a particular food or condiment is preferred or disliked. Maybe if we added tomato sauce, this would radically change the food we are serving. We reach often enough for pickles, chutneys and sauces to enhance flavour and therefore stimulate taste buds further, so why can't we apply the same principles to those we are feeding? Very profoundly handicapped children and adults are not going to ask us to 'pass the ketchup' and they're not going to complain about too much sugar or too little salt or not enough jam. We have to try and find ways of being able to arrive at what it really is that they do like.

Meal times are such important parts of the day, and it is because they are so important that we ought to pay more attention to them. If food is going to be served at all, then it really ought to be presented in a way that makes it exciting to eat. How often have we found ourselves in positions of having to spoon feed a meal that quite frankly disturbs us to look at? But this is an area that we can do something about — given that we want to that is.

Feeding times are educational. Verbal information about types of foods can be given — signing can be involved. Explanations about what is coming next is not only necessary but is vital preparation for the different tastes involved.

VARIETY

It is incredibly boring to have the same food day in, day out. Likewise it is equally as boring to have the same beverages and drinks. There are too many choices available on the market today for any of us to be unadventurous in what we offer to those in our care. For a variety in flavour not to be offered only makes us incredibly boring too. It is quite amazing how far one orange will go! Peeled and pipped, and cut into segments, it can be given to everyone. Just writing about it sends my taste buds into action!

As eating and drinking are such frequent and vital aspects of our lives, then given some thought it will not take long to arrive at a suitable and practicable list of foods and drinks that can be tried out with handicapped individuals and groups. But like all things, it needs careful thought and planning — and of course the effort on the practitioners part to implement it.

7   Being Realistic

Movement

If the handicapped person in our care is ambulant, then it automatically should follow that a certain amount of movement exercises ought to be part of their programme. Not having the initiative or the incentive to move around of their own accord, then the responsibility must be ours to ensure that movement is encouraged. Walking to and from the toilet, or to and from the dining room, or to and from the bedroom is not the type of movement I am referring to here. I am concerned in this section with the types of movement that we instigate over and above the normal moving around that occurs during the normal day. I would like to concentrate on what it is that we are asking the handicapped person to do, rather than on the complexities and uses of equipment that may be at our disposal.

RATIONALE

First it must be established that having some form of movement is important to the overall individual programme. Apart from the obvious reasons for improving circulation and general muscle tone in limbs, there are added advantages. Teamwork, stimulus, excitement, new experiences are just a few bonuses that we can give to the handicapped person in our care.

Choosing the right time of the day to set up movement activities can be crucial to the well running and enjoyment of such an activity. Directly after lunch is hardly the time to expect anyone to feel at their most energetic. Similarly, at the end of the day, worn out by all the other activities, there will not be the motivation needed to produce the best results. Obviously the time chosen depends very much on the routine of the setting. But it should be considered that the best time of the day is the time that suits the people involved — the handicapped people involved. In my own experiences, I have found that more progress can be made in the mornings than at any other time. It is an arguable point, but the majority of people are at their best first thing in the morning.

THINK BEFORE YOU SPEAK

I do not wish to insult the reader by suggesting how many hoops ought to be placed in a straight line, or how many bean bags ought to be encouraged to be thrown in the bucket, or which peice of music should be chosen to 'sway like trees' to — but I would suggest that whatever activity we set up, we are fully aware of exactly what it is we are asking others to do.

For example:

'Pick up the ball and pass it to me.'

By breaking down this very simple task into stages, we can see how complex it really is.

First stage   Pick up the ball:
   (1) Pick up of verbal and visual (if given) instruction and interpretation.
   (2) Hand–eye contact and location of ball.
   (3) Movement of arm and body and balance.
   (4) Maintain hand–eye contact if ball is located and picked up.
   (5) Concentration and dexterity to hold onto ball.

Second stage   Pass it to me:
   (6) Interpretation of instruction.
   (7) Maintain concentration and dexterity skills.
   (8) Hand–eye contact — location of receiver of object.
   (9) Maintain balance.
   (10) Involve appropriate arm movement to propel ball.
   (11) Focus on target.
   (12) Coordinate movements to achieve throw.

It is very, very complicated. Although we would probably never give this a second thought, by asking for such a simple task to be completed we are in effect asking for at least twelve actions and impulses to be reacted upon correctly. Can we reasonably expect a profoundly handicapped person to accomplish such a task with relative ease? Because it may appear to be simple to our ears and through our eyes, can we assume that this will be the case for others?

Before we set up equipment, we must look more closely at what it is we are asking people to do. We must also have very clear ideas as to the objectives that we are setting. Exercise and movement sessions are hard work, not just for handicapped people but for workers as well. Why waste excess energy in complicated manoeuvres which only add to the confusion when with a little thought the activity can be so much more beneficial?

Again it is back to planning. An activity can never be too simple. Better that it is within the reach of those it is intended for than it being a pie-in-the-sky task. Making it more complex and intricate can wait until the basics are well established first. Introduce equipment using its proper name. Allow handicapped people time to explore. Do they want to touch it? Smell it? Feel the texture? Give them opportunities to experiment with it. Can it be lifted? Can they get into it? All these things are so very important. You know what it is — but do they?

If an object is felt to be accessible, then it will appear as being safe. It can be quite anxiety-provoking to be suddenly confronted with a piece of equipment that has never been seen before, and then be asked to do unsafe things with it. We have had the opportunities to examine everything — our handicapped sector of the community have not. There is nothing to lose by giving this time — and everything to gain.

KEEP IT SIMPLE

If the activity is part of the programme, then provide the consistency that is required by always starting off the session using the same 'game'. This will quickly establish the ritual and safety needed for the handicapped person to feel comfortable about the work that will follow. Confidence levels will rise, which is just what is needed for all the complicated things you have planned out for future sessions.

As confidence levels are improved, so will the trust in you. Without these two important elements, nothing will be achieved. If you can prove that you are not going to spring dangerous and complicated things at people, then you will become a very safe person to work with, but you have to prove that what you ask is not impossible and will not cause distress. As with many aspects of the work, results will be more forthcoming if we adopt the slowly, slowly approach. Once the basic concepts have been grasped and are attainable, we can then start to build and add in the complexities. Presenting new experiences all the time will do very little for developing relationships and raising confidence levels. Variety is important, but familiarity is imperative. The prevailing theme is one of awareness, not only that of the handicapped person but the awareness of ourselves in our attitude to and how we go about our work.

Getting Wet

The ideal situation is to have access to swimming pool, hydrotherapy pool and space for water play within the Unit. The provision of all three varies depending on the resources available in each area, but this section will hopefully provide the reader with some ideas as to how 'water play' can be used as an effective therapeutic measure.

HYDROTHERAPY

Hydrotherapy pools and equipment not only aid mobility but are also great fun places to be. Apart from the therapeutic value, in terms of physical activity, there is also the advantage gained by change of environment. Hydrotherapy pools facilitate the opportunity to get really close to profoundly handicapped people. Of course you can have the same degree of closeness in any pool area, but hydrotherapy pools are far more private. The water temperature is always constant and

should always be warm, both of which are very conducive to the needs of the profoundly handicapped person.

While it must be remembered that the water is a facilitator for freedom, the amount or degree of physiotherapy that is employed is really quite arbitrary. The important thing is that the experience is an enjoyable one. If the handicapped person is so relaxed by the water that they fall asleep, then that has as much therapeutic value as physiotherapy can have. Not having the noise levels that are common to swimming pools, it is possible to do a variety of awareness techniques in the hydrotherapy pool. One that I use frequently is to submerge a plastic container to the side of the head of the person I am supporting, and then watch for reactions as the water bubbles. Another is to pour water from a container at different angles and to observe if there is any indication of the person trying to establish where the noise is coming from.

Hydrotherapy pools are great fun. An activity list is not really necessary as lots of ideas just fall into place quite naturally. Being there is the most important thing.

SWIMMING POOLS

Trips to the local swimming pool, where facilities are shared

by the general public, can be extremely beneficial for handicapped people. This is obviously an activity that involves
more than one person. In establishing such a programme, at
the outset, the obstacles seem almost insurmountable: cost,
transport, helpers being just a few examples. From experience,
cost and transport are excuses given for not being able to
start a programme; in actual fact, major problems are concerned with dressing and undressing.

COST

Using any pool will inevitably incur expense. Most local
authorities have some arrangement with schools with regard
to payment. Money does not change hands — bits of paper
merely move from one building to another via the internal
post. If the activity is to be a regular weekly affair, then the
need to establish this as having its own budget is essential.
To do this may not be easy, but it can be done.

Reasonable arguments can be put forward about the com-
parative costs of other activities (often for the more able),
good examples being football pitch hire, outings, film hire,
and the like. A clear outline of the aims of the activity and
the obvious benefit that will be derived from it will go a long
way towards winning the hearts of the purse string holders.
Every effort ought to be made to follow through this channel
before you start. Once you have raised funds from other
quarters, the battle to get it put on budget will become harder.

If this fails, do not give up! Rally support from the community. Local press, local councillors, local voluntary organisations may be able to help. Jumble sales have been held for
far less worthy causes! Parent–Staff Associations may be able
to come up with some good money-raising schemes. One
thing is certain, money will not be forthcoming if you sit
back and wait for it to arrive. A belief in the activity, and
high energy levels to see through what you have started, will
determine its success or failure.

TRANSPORT

To get this side of things organised is not easy. Very often a ramp ambulance or specially designed minibus to cater for wheelchair people may be necessary. If the local authority has got the resources of specialist transport, you can put money on them being in use *all the time*. Every other agency that is using this facility will have presented a good case for their use. You must do the same.

HELP!

Taking profoundly handicapped groups swimming warrants a member of staff from their area to go with them. This will deplete staff levels and automatically set off heated discussion on the priorities of 'who gets left behind'. You do not have to look very far for help. Parents seeing the opportunity for such an exciting activity will fall over themselves to volunteer! There is a time and place for emotional blackmail, and this is one. Local voluntary organisations nearly always have people on their books who would love to help, but they have to know about the activity and they have to be approached.

PLAN OF ACTION

You are not about to start World War III, but your preparations must be exact, in the event that once the ball starts rolling, this may be what it feels as if is happening. Make long lists of the advantages and disadvantages of the activity. Be positive and realistic in your arguments for presenting the case. Go and personally talk to staff members at the swimming pool. It is not enough to speak to a sympathetic manager — you need to know how poolside personnel feel about your proposals. Reactions may be mixed. Some teachers think it is an excellent exercise in providing their pupils with the opportunity of working alongside handicapped people — but unfortunately there are those who do not. But you need to know how the land lies first.

HOMEWORK

Rummage through case notes for any history of swimming

activity outside of the school, centre or hospital programme — possibly with parents at weekends or on holiday. Approach these parents informally and get their opinion as to how they would feel about 'swimming' as an activity. Convince them of your intent, and get their support. Make sure one of them is a member of the Parent–Teacher Association, or similar, and ask them to put it on the Agenda for the next meeting. Minutes usually have a wide circulation, and in no time at all half the community will have some idea of what's afoot! Establish the views of the 'powers that be' and other staff members, and try to get the topic 'aired' at appropriate meetings. Time permitting, go and get first-hand experience of it working somewhere else with similar groups. Take copious notes and talk to people who 'do it all the time'.

Use internal channels to establish what is going to be easy to get and what is not. Go and talk to your local friendly paper, with all the facts, and play on their community mindedness. Leave your name and telephone number, and make sure that you stay in for at least one week following its publication! Different authorities have different guidelines, in terms of policy and safety aspects. Check this out at the *beginning* and ensure that you are complying with what is in operation in your area.

ONCE THERE

The water is a disguiser of many handicaps. Any differences that there are between helper and handicapped are not so obvious in the water, and certainly are not so noticeable — a situation that seldom occurs on dry land. Discovering buoyancy is quite an experience. Water facilitates a sense of freedom that can never be equalled on land. It is obvious from facial reactions whether the activity is an enjoyable one or not. Nine times out of ten, the squeals are motivated by pleasure, rather than the reverse.

An important aspect of water play is that it enables close physical contact between those involved. At the very least, it facilitates hand holding. On dry land, there may be reluctance to allow any sort of 'closeness' to occur — but the water dictates very different terms. It is also an opportunity to combine groups of varying abilities. More able people get an enormous amount of satisfaction from helping rather than being helped. Not having the restriction of clothing, straps and support wedges must bring about an unbelievable sense of freedom. Games can be played in the water which are as pleasurable for the helpers as they are for the group concerned.

Increasing confidence levels in the water will have added advantages in that there will be raised confidence levels in other areas too. Having the opportunity to work closely with different people will help to develop skills to form relationships more easily.

There are a variety of aids on the market to assist buoyancy and create safety boundaries. Before spending lots of money on what might appear to be the right equipment, it is worth taking the time to investigate this area more fully. The most commonly used aids are inflated armbands. For small children just learning to swim, these can be an invaluable aid. However, for the handicapped child and adult, I am not at all in favour of them being used. They are a great disadvantage in many ways. The tendency is usually to inflate them fully and, once in position on the upper arm, they are not only uncomfortable but they also raise the arms to an unnatural position. Although the water will support the body, having arms raised in this position will cause discomfort after a few minutes. (Try it and see.) Arm discs are far more comfortable and therapeutic. They are flat, and can be used in any combination. Two or three can be worn at the same time. They are more cost effective as they last longer. There is also the added safety factor in that you need never worry about them 'going down'. They are easy to store and can be played with in the water as well as worn.

Float boards have a variety of uses, and can be bought at reasonable prices. They are manufactured in different sizes, colours and shapes. The more appealing the colour and design, the more fun they will provide. But plain white ones can be decorated with patterns and motifs.

Dumb-bell floats are probably the most successful aids I have used. They are wide enough to be used as a walking aid and can be held at arm's length without interfering with balance, and yet are light and not at all cumbersome in the water. Each piece can be used independently.

Polystyrene blocks stitched into bathing costumes create situations of 'false buoyancy'. Having removed them, however, I have found the blocks to have a far greater beneficial use. They are the perfect size to hold in hands.

Rubber rings or inflated rings rank very low on the equipment scene. I personally find them dangerous and would never use them with handicapped groups. They provide no safety in support. For someone with physical problems, they can tip the body so easily, and accidents are sure to happen.

Table tennis balls are an extremely useful aid. They are small enough to be blown across the water. Sponges can be used in a manner of ways. Pretending to have a shower, getting washed and so on are not only reinforcing social skills that are taught back at base, but also provide the opportunity for more water skills activities.

Lilos can be used — but with caution. It serves no purpose to cause such anxiety in getting onto the lilo that they are then so agitated you cannot do anything else. But if it is possible to use this piece of equipment, then it can bring a lot of enjoyment.

Basically, there are a number of things that can be used — their success depends on how well you know your groups. Slowly, slowly always gets better results than rushing things.

There is equal opportunity for not using any equipment at all. If funds are not available, then this does not mean that the activity will be a failure. Singing and action rhymes can be used as extensively in the water as they can out. Ring-a-ring of roses, with variations for endings — 'all blow bubbles', 'bob right down' — is not only providing a fun environment but developing water confidence skills. Working in pairs, holding hands, facing each other and 'bunny hopping' across the pool can incorporate races and water skills. Circle games with each person numbered either one or two. All the number ones lie on their backs and then kick their legs and splash. This is nearly always seen as being safe as there is someone on each side of them holding their hands and giving gentle encouragement. Then ask the number twos to do the same thing — and see which group makes the biggest splash.

Simple activities such as walking round in a circle can go a long way towards increasing confidence levels. Making a train and doing the Conga are all very good group activities.

Apart from the group activities and the one-to-one work, there should always be time allowed for free play. Keeping observation keen, wherever possible, opportunity for exploring and experimenting ought to be encouraged.

For those who have a fear of the water or just 'don't want to do it', they too should be included in this activity in an observing sense. Standing or sitting on the pool side for some people is as therapeutic as 'getting wet'. Ball games can include people on the pool side — there's nothing in the rules that says everyone has to be in the water. The more immobile the person, the more likely the possibility of shivering. Don't be put off. Ten minutes water time is better than no water time at all. Remember, the aim is to promote enjoyment, not to reach Olympic standards.

SPECIFIC PROBLEMS

For most people in a Special Care Unit there are added complications such as heart complaints, epilepsy and so on. It is always advisable to check with the GP first, to ensure that the activity will be beneficial and not detrimental to the handicapped person's well-being. In the event that they are included in the programme, then at all times one helper should be allocated to each person in this category, to ensure that they are being 'watched' at all times.

GOLDEN RULES

Safety comes first.

There must be an activity leader. This person ought to be on the pool side throughout the session, for maximum observations, and also to be able to be seen by everyone. All movements ought to be directed through the leader. If someone needs to leave the pool to go to the toilet, then the leader must be aware of this.

All helpers must have duties delegated to them and to know at all times what is expected of them.

Rope off the area of the pool you are using. This makes it easier for your group, and also for the lifeguards and other pool staff.

The leader ought to have check cards on everyone involved in the activity, outlining details, including medication and allergies. In the event that an accident should occur, and admission to hospital is necessary, then it will save precious time if the vital information is at hand, without having to phone to base for it.

Keep records of achievement — no matter how minimal — and reward progress as it occurs, with badges and certificates. Involve more able clients in the design of certificates. Have a club badge made. They're not expensive and you owe it to the group to acknowledge that they do belong to a swimming club.

Never underestimate what can be done.

Keep photographic records of the activity. Visitors and parents will be delighted with what they see.

Most importantly — enjoy it.

WATER PLAY

This is an activity that can take place almost anywhere. Buckets, bowls and a few floatable objects are all that are needed. As with all activities, never underestimate capabilities. Despite the severity of the handicap, explanations should always be given before the activity starts. Where groups are ambulant or mobile, then including them in the setting up of the activity is very important. It can be quite distressing to have a bucket of water suddenly appear in front of you for no apparent reason. Take them with you when collecting equipment.

ONE TO ONE

Tapping, feeling, smelling, listening and watching water can be stimulating. Gentle encouragement will soon result in spontaneous play. It may be necessary at first to hold hands and introduce them to water very slowly and gradually. Use objects that float and sink. Encourage them to watch what happens to each object. Allow them time to experiment and explore. Never rush things. Remember to include vocabulary that is simple, but not boring. Ensure that when an object is picked up it has a name. By introducing someone else into the game, you are encouraging them to form relationships and to share. Remember, there is enough room in a bucket of water for more than two hands! Sponges can be great fun. They leave little to the imagination with regard to what can be done with them.

Obviously, the bigger the receptacle, the more involvement can be accommodated. Plastic troughs can be used on tables or the floor. (It can be very soothing to sit with feet immersed in water.) Caution should be exercised with wet floors. Support wedges can be used to prop people up so that they can lie on their stomachs and dangle their hands into bowls of water. Water play does not have to be done sitting or standing.

If a patio or garden is available, then the next step is the paddling pool — weather permitting of course. Plastic lemonade bottles and washing-up liquid bottles can be used quite safely. Listening to water rushing up and down a half-filled bottle has been known to cause great delight. Plastic ice cubes, designed for chilling gin and tonics, are colourful enough and small enough to have their place in bucket water play.

ADVANTAGES OF WATER PLAY

Encourages movement of hands.
Encourages interaction.
Encourages hand–eye coordination.
Is fun for all.
Facilitates observation for others (if enough pleasurable squeals are produced, this may attract others to want to know what is going on).
Enables clients to be active.
Allows exploration and experimentation.
Heightens sense awareness.

DISADVANTAGES

Everyone gets soaked.
The floor gets wet.

Always tell parents if clients are likely to go home with wet shoes. In my experience, they have always been pleased with the wetness rather than upset about it. It adds to the enjoyment if staff are appropriately dressed. It is no good the group being in swimsuits and expecting them to take the plunge if staff are not prepared to do the same.

If space permits, then two or three pools can be very advantageous. This allows more people to be involved at any one time. It also enables personality clashing to be kept to a minimum. It is an activity that everyone can do together and it helps to bridge gaps — which can only enhance relationships.

At home, garden hoses can quickly fill paddling pools, topped up by some hot water to keep the temperature bearable. Sitting in a pool breaks the monotony of sitting in a wheelchair. Washing equipment can be done as a group activity, and turned into a game, rather than it being a chore. Watering the plants is best done outside — so it really does not matter if the water gets everywhere but on the plants. The feeling of being involved and doing something is what is important.

POINTS TO REMEMBER

Safety comes first.

Expensive equipment is not always necessary.

Immobile people will get cold quickly. Unless the weather is baking hot, be aware of the first signs of shivering.

Poor concentration spans may warrant just a few minutes play and then disinterest. Go along with this. Leave the equipment where it is — you can always go back to it.

A few minutes water time is better than none at all.

Think twice about throwing away objects that may float (kitchen utensil set). Mention to friends and colleagues that you are on the lookout for old towels and swimsuits. You'll be amazed at what gets thrown at you!

Yawn, Yawn — Boring, Boring

There is little that can be done with a person if they are asleep. The first thing that needs to be established is the reason why they are asleep. Sleeping is a very good method to employ so as not to have to do anything. But it is also an excellent way of passing the time if what there is to do is boring and unstimulating. Side effects of drugs apart, it is reasonable to expect an awakened state during the day. After meals many people do have tendencies to nap — this is normal. But what about times during the day when, given all these factors, people still sleep? The sleeping child looks peaceful, resting and relaxed. It is hard to bring oneself to wake him up, knowing that when awake, he may suffer discomfort and distress during the change of position. So very often, the child is left to sleep on.

A sensible compromise needs to be reached very early on in the programme and routine, so that stimulation is given despite the sleepy state. If the child can eventually learn to appreciate that being awake is not always boring, that sometimes there are quite a number of exciting and stimulating things going on, then there will not be such a tendency to want to sleep all the time. If, on the other hand, the sleepy state is encouraged, this only perpetuates the sleepiness so that gradually this then becomes a very hard pattern to break at all.

Practitioners must work towards finding a balance, one that is suitable and applicable to individual needs. All sleep and no play makes Jack very boring. If Jack is that boring, then this will add yet another barrier between himself and the practitioner preventing any possible work from being carried out. Needless to say, if practitioners then become completely surrounded by boring sleepy groups, they too will pick up these feelings and end up being boring themselves. It can be a vicious circle. Now you don't want people to think you are boring do you?

8   Being Creative

Music

The value of music in its broadest context can be of tremendous benefit and enjoyment to us all. We use it in a variety of ways — listening to music for relaxation, participating, playing an instrument, as part of an audience, as a distraction, to dance and move to, and so on. Music as entertainment has been part of our history, and is a very important part of our lives. For the many rituals that all cultures need to have, music plays a major role. We have special songs and special music for different occasions.

THE ABUSE OF MUSIC

When there is an element of choice, we tend to be selective about our own choice of music. At the end of a hard and stressful day, when all we want to do is sit quietly and relax, we would hardly welcome a rousing chorus or two of 'Land of Hope and Glory'. Similarly, if we want something to listen to that will cheer us up, we would be unlikely to choose a dirge. There are times when we choose to have music playing in the background, and times when we need not to have it there. Whatever our preferences to time and place, we can to a certain extent choose the category or type of music that we want, when we want it.

For immobile handicapped people there is often very little choice. The choice made is nearly always that of whoever happens to be with them at the time, but it is rarely theirs. So we must be very aware of what it is that we are really doing when we switch on the radio in the morning. Has a handicapped person asked us to do it? Why do we switch the radio on? Is it because it is there? Is it because we work better if music is playing?

As with painting, music is an activity that is often used to occupy people rather than providing a stimulating and educational environment for them. Very often it is because little thought is given to what it is we are trying to do with music that leads to non-productive and unstimulating sessions. It can be seen as an added bonus if a member of staff can play an instrument as well. Because they can sing and play, this seems to be the criterion and rationale for 'doing' music. The group gathered round the player is encouraged to join in regardless.

A lot can be said for rousing choruses of 'The wheels on the bus go round and round', but only if it is used appropriately. Similarly, 'Simon, Simon, where are you? Here I am, Here I am, How do you do' might not be appropriate to everyone.

Major abuse of time set aside for music sessions must be when the percussion instruments are handed out and the group are then encouraged to play whatever it is they are holding in their hands at the time, be it drum, cymbals, tambourine or whatever. The out-of-tune discordant noise that follows could never be described as musical — it is often horrendous. It is disharmonious noise that is far from pleasing to the ear. It is not enjoyable and it is certainly not stimulating — so why is it done? Partly, I think the answer to this is to do with using equipment. 'If the tambourines and drums are available, then they ought to be used.' Rather than use them just for the sake of using them, we ought to look more closely at how best they can be used.

TRIANGLES, FINGER BELLS AND BELLS

All these produce soft sounds and are quiet instruments. They can be used on their own or to accompany background 'soft' music. They can be used in conjunction with vocabulary build-up of the word 'soft', incorporating items and objects that are also 'soft'. The therapist can play the instrument out of sight of the handicapped person and observe response. For instance, if bells are jingled, just behind the left ear, will the person turn to the left to identify it? Is the sound heard? Can the sound be identified by name? Does the sound appear to stimulate interest? Triangles involve coordination skills, as do most instruments, but can be successfully played with little help.

PERCUSSION

Tambourines are multipurpose, but are more difficult to hold correctly. Castanets, chimebells, sticks, xylophones, in fact all percussion instruments, are all useful pieces of equipment — if used wisely.

MUSICAL VARIETY

The collection of records and tapes should include all types of music — vocal, instrumental, classical, jazz, western, modern, and so on. Music that can be played to relax to, as well as music to move around to, should be varied and incorporate as many interests as is possible. Marches can be used for 'marching', lullabies for sleeping. Having the same music to listen to all the time is boring and frustrating.

Rhyming games can be played successfully with language activities, using simple tunes to reinforce vocabulary. Diane has difficulty/reluctance in communicating with the spoken word, but has an awful lot to say if the same words can be set to music. When wanting to introduce new words to her vocabulary, I try and find a song that has the word included and just sing it to her, and it works every time.

Music is a valuable learning instrument. Used wisely and appropriately, it can assist the therapist to broaden the horizons of the handicapped person, and open yet more windows on their world.

Painting

Within us all lie creative capabilities. As each person is an individual, so then are their respective creative talents. Having an eye for detail — the ability to capture 'life' and depict it in paint — for some is a talent that is obvious to the observer. To say that the natural talent or flair is missing must not lead us to presume that there are no creative or artistic traits within that person. When we create something, we are in effect projecting something of ourselves onto our finished product. The importance does not lie with the artistic merits achieved, but with the creativity involved.

The restrictions that handicapped people live with narrow their experiences and limit their development. For those involved with their care falls the responsibility for facilitating opportunities for free expression — and this can be brought about by using paint as the medium. Working in the field of profound handicap, we must try to provide the opportunities for creative instincts to be first found, and then developed and explored.

Art can be relaxing and pleasurable. It is a medium of expression that can be employed to assist the learning process associated with new materials and environment. Art can broaden horizons, increase awareness of surroundings and bring new knowledge to the handicapped person. It is experiential and can contribute to understanding and enjoyment of life. The therapist must use the medium in an educational way, as opposed to occupational, and in carefully structured sessions objectives can be easily achieved.

Mention painting and everyone automatically thinks of brushes and easels. When working with profoundly handicapped people, activities that involve the 'holding' of something are very often the activities that they are prevented from doing. 'We can't do that because John can't hold a brush.' 'We can't do that because Susan can't see', and so on. A long list of excuses that are really the reasons why the worker does not want to be involved in something messy.

Setting up the activity can be part of a guessing game as to what is going to happen next. When the more able members of the group start collecting the necessary pieces of equipment, this can often lead the less able members feeling left out. It is yet another activity that they cannot join in, but by making this into a game, you are at least doing something about relieving their isolation. Try and include as many members of the group as is practicable and possible to set up the activity. As with all activities, an awareness of time is important. It takes time to set the activity up, and even more time to clear things away. Make sure that having made allowance for this, there is still time to paint.

BE ADVENTUROUS BUT REALISTIC

Staffing levels must be considered. It is all very well to have your wonderful ideas, but none of them will be possible if you have not got the staff to carry them out. Position tables and chairs *before* you start to make a mess. There is nothing more chaotic than trying to rearrange furniture and people with water and paint spilling everywhere! People do not have to be grouped according to ability. It may be best to have two people working together on one table at the same time as another six on the next table. You know your group best.

MESS IS INEVITABLE

There is nothing wrong with making a mess! It is therapeutic and it is fun. Parents will rarely be annoyed when their

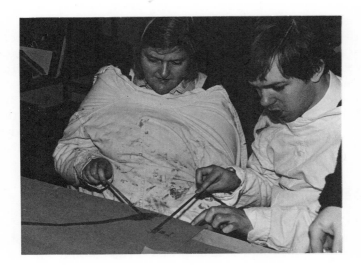

children return home covered in paint, if they know that they thoroughly enjoyed doing it. But sensible precautions can be made to keep the mess to a minimum. It is advisable to put on overalls, or old shirts, before you start. In my experience, this has not stopped paint from getting everywhere — but it certainly does help to protect clothing.

CHOOSING MATERIALS

Painting is not an expensive activity. The cost of paper varies depending on the quality. If you have to beg and plead for paper, try some of the following:

  (i) Yellow paper used in X-ray departments. Endless supplies are available — all you have to do is ask.
 (ii) Computer printout sheets.
(iii) Newspapers.
 (iv) Posters that are no longer needed. (Supermarkets are excellent places to ask for these.)

Paint can be bought in various forms. Again it depends on your budget as to what you will purchase. Ready mixed paint, in plastic bottles, has a fairly thick consistency, which makes it economical and also saves time to set up. But powder paints are fun to mix. Blocks are also useful, but you may find that they are too small to handle for the more profoundly handicapped child and adult.

Useful pieces of equipment, which are in the long term very economical, are storage pots. They are made of plastic, have stoppers to prevent spillage and are easily stored. Because they can be sealed, this allows you to use the paint mixed in your own time, without having to waste any.

Palates are an added expense — unnecessarily. I find that they are too small, and when coordination is difficult, they tend to add to the problem rather than help it. Margarine pots and serving trays are by far the best substitutes.

BRUSHES

Paint brushes can be awkward things to hold. They are invariably long and thin, and well beyond the grasping power of most multi-handicapped people. This should not be a problem though, unless you are wanting the finished article to look like a Turner or a Picasso! Paint brushes do not have to have long handles. Cut down the handles so that they are half the size. Polystyrene balls can be glued to the ends to make them more attractive and easier to hold. Folding fingers around the handles can give encouragement. It may be that unless you physically hold the hand holding the brush, then nothing will happen. Just because a handicapped person has lost the use of a limb does not mean to say that you can assume that it no longer can be moved or used. It can be used with your help.

Toothbrushes, nail brushes, washing-up brushes, scrubbing brushes, household paint brushes are all better designed to be held than the average artist's brush. They are all items that are easily obtainable. Most households, at some point, are on the verge of throwing some of them away — all you have to do is make sure that they are thrown at you!

ALTERNATIVES

Sponges are multipurpose. They can be cut to the size required, and can produce quite startling effects. Fingers are marvellous, as are toes, knees, elbows and heels. Painting should never be confined to just fingers and hands. If a part of the body can be used, use it. Use cardboard — it is stiff enough to hold and move. Once it gets soggy, of course, it will have to be replaced.

BODY PAINTS

The majority of paint on the market is non-toxic, so there is not a problem of worrying about it getting in mouths and up noses and causing damage. There are, however, a number of paints available specifically designed for body painting. If a person is so handicapped that movement is impossible, then try painting their face and then showing them what you have done in a hand mirror. Better still, support them so they can watch what you are doing throughout. Be prepared for them not liking it! Just because you think it is a good idea doesn't mean that they will! Painting in the bath can be great fun, providing the brush is soft! Most body paints are soapy, so you can kill two birds with one stone, and make bath time a more enjoyable activity.

Always try and involve as many of the group as is possible. Even if some group members cannot join in unless a worker is with them on a one-to-one basis, if they are positioned in such a way that they are physically part of the group, this will enable them to feel that they are involved in what is going on. Severity of handicap should never be the excuse for not participating in an activity.

SEEING AND HEARING PAINTING

Watching the transformation of colours can be exciting. If people are unable to mix colours for themselves, they can watch others mixing them. Have you ever heard paints plop? You should try it! I recall one session, where we did not actually get around to doing any painting — we simply spent the time 'plopping' paint intead!

Brushes of all sizes make sounds. Compare the differences from tapping a brush on the table when it is dry, listening to it in water, and again when it has paint on it on paper. Mixing paint has a sound to it. Powder paints are great fun to listen to. If someone is blind, they may be able to hear the paint. Loss of vision should not mean that painting is inaccessible.

BLOWING PAINT

Blowing is a difficult skill to teach. For some strange reason showing by example rarely gets results. But if the concept is understood, then straws can be brought in to make it more enjoyable. If this is impossible, but the handicapped person is able to hold on to something, either with or without help, then there are other items that can be used.

    (i)   Hairdryers. Caution must be exercised and a watchful eye kept on the direction that they are pointed in, but the results are worth while.

    (ii)   Bicycle pumps, foot pumps, balloon pumps. These items leave little to the imagination, but care needs to be taken. Used appropriately they can produce exciting and enjoyable results.

For some people there is a tendency to start painting at one particular point on the paper. This may be in the middle to work outwards, or the painting may just be confined to one side, or top or bottom of the paper. The size of paper needs to be considered, so that it suits the needs of the individual. If you wish to develop this aspect further, then the paper can be divided into sections to encourage full use of the area to be painted.

IDEAS TO GET YOU GOING

Objects of all kinds can be used, coffee jar lids, plastic shapes from puzzles, toy cars, plastic cups, combs, material, buttons — the list is endless.

TABLE-TOP PAINTING

Mix the paint so that it is very watery, and put it into a container in which objects can be easily submerged, for instance, a pudding bowl. Dip the object into the paint, then dab it all over the table-top. The results can be amazing. If the paint used for this particular exercise is watery, then it makes life a lot easier when it is time to clear away!

SENSORY PAINTING

Pour thick paint onto a tray and then pour tiny polystyrene balls onto the paint and watch what happens. Squeals of delight are guaranteed as people watch the balls changing colour. Rubbing the paint over the balls stimulates sensory perception. If the paint is thick enough, then the balls will stick to the fingers and hopefully encourage the use of the other hand to remove the 'mess'. You can then experiment with different shapes, and introduce different colours.

Mix white flour and water until you have a workable dough. Involve the group as much as you can. The more able can pour the water into the bowl — but everyone can experience how the dough feels. Roll out the dough with a rolling pin (not too thinly) and using biscuit or cake cutters cut out different shapes. Paint the shapes liberally, then turn them upside down onto paper. Pat them gently and then lift the pastry and you will see the pattern left on the paper.

The shapes can be anything you want them to be. Some lovely pictures have been made using this method. There are a variety of objects that have other uses than those for which they were originally intended. Balls, of all shapes and textures, can produce exciting patterns if rolled over paper covered in paint. All that is needed is a gentle shove across the table. Pouring paint onto paper and just watching to see what happens to it can be very stimulating. Similarly, pouring paint onto paper and then folding the paper over and back, allowing it to dry, has created butterflies with a difference.

NET CURTAINS

These are always available at jumble sales and oddments are cheap to buy. Place netting on paper or staple to paper if this is easier. Simply paint over the netting. Remove netting for end product. The more intricate the pattern on the netting, the more intricate the painting. There is plenty of scope with this activity for experimenting with colours and shapes.

KITCHEN GLOVES

These are very easy to use. The gloves inevitably will have some form of pattern, and this can be easily transferred to paper or card by simply wearing the glove, dipping the glove into paint, and then pressing the glove onto the paper. This is ideal for those who hate getting dirty.

TIN FOIL

Apart from the difference in texture and the fact that the foil is shiny and can make a noise, this is a good contrast activity. Paint the foil and then press onto the paper. Lift the foil for result.

GLUE

Glue can change the consistency of the paint quite remarkably and relatively quickly. Although it can be extremely messy, it is yet another way that painting can be made to be a little different. Once dry, it leaves a thickening and three-dimensional effect, which can be used in other activities using touch. Sprinkling sawdust onto glue and then, when dry, painting over, can bring pictures 'away' from the paper.

FROM THE GARDEN

By carefully choosing items from the garden, you can easily bring two activities together. Collect leaves, petals, cones and stalks, when out on a nature walk, as these are all items that can be used in art sessions later.

The value of reinforcement of language and other relative aspects cannot be stressed enough. This is an ideal option to link activities in an educational way. Leaves can be painted and pressed onto paper. They can also be used to paint around, and by using different types of leaves, experiments can be made with size and shape.

MATERIAL

Hessian, felt, fur, chiffon, tweed, in fact all pieces of material that can be acquired for little financial outlay are useful objects to paint. Introducing the different types of material will not only produce varying results but also provide new tactile and sensory experiences.

CORRUGATED CARDBOARD, RUBBER AND PAPER

Cardboard linings for boxes are often corrugated and are ideal for making new patterns on paper. Similarly, slip mats for baths and rubber car mats can produce startling results when painted and then pressed onto paper. By cutting up the items to a workable size, a variety of patterns can be made.

STENCILS

There are numerous types of stencil that can be bought, but they are also easy to make. They are economical and great fun. You can also incorporate vocabulary reinforcement as you use them.

Take strong card/paper/newspaper/cardboard/magazine pages, anything that is available, and cut out a simple shape, for example a face. Make holes in the shape for eyes, ears, nose and mouth. Place the stencil on the paper and help to paint over the holes. Lift off the stencil, and you should have the pattern underneath.

Let the group experiment with different colours so that they can see the differences that can be made. Magazines are full of lovely bright pictures that can be used as a stencil base. Try and match up the pictures so that they are things that can be related to. If one of the boys likes cars, then make the stencil out of a picture of a car, leaving the wheels as the parts to be painted in. If it is someone's birthday, then use a picture of a cake, with the candles to be coloured in.

It may be that there is a group project in operation and certain 'pieces' need to be painted. We all know that it is much quicker to do it ourselves, but try to find the time for the group to be involved. Creating something and being able to see it in its completed state is an incredibly rewarding experience. If you want your group to put any value on what they are doing, then you have to put value on it too. Display everything. If you've got it — flaunt it! Send paintings home to parents, so that they can see how the time has been spent. This is also proof of why their child started off the day in blue, and came home covered in red bits!

When I was interviewing Sandra's parents, they showed me her room, and two of the walls were covered in her paintings. They said that they liked the idea of Sandra being able to lie in bed, looking at the work she had done. 'Were she a normal child, this wall might be covered in pop posters! Aren't we lucky?!'

There really are no rules and regulations governing art sessions. All that is needed is a bit of space, some time and a sense of adventure.

Sand

Sand is a wonderful sensory stimulant. It is easy to come by — most builders will part with a bucket full! Any receptacle, irrespective of size, can be used: large troughs, old zinc baths, trays, buckets, bowls, plastic cups — the list goes on and on. A few extra bits of equipment can make the activity more lively, though they are far from being necessary. I refer here to objects such as spades, sieves, brushes, rakes, and so on.

FEELING SAND

Simply moving hands through the sand can be a pleasurable experience. Trying to get someone to watch their hands moving around not only warrants some degree of concentration, but it also facilitates the feeling of a very different texture. If someone is rather hesitant about the activity, then slowly introducing them to the sand can be done by gently pouring sand onto their fingers.

NOW YOU SEE IT — NOW YOU DON'T

Hiding favourite objects in the sand is a very good method of assessing concentration spans and memory recall. But please note that this won't work if the objects that are hidden are not worth searching for! But there might be a favourite ball, brick or book that would fit the bill here for these purposes.

WET SAND

By wetting the sand, not only does the texture change, in terms of temperature and touch, but it also enables other things to be done. The sand can then be easily moulded into certain shapes. Possibly with the use of moulds, some models can be made. Watching the sand change format is a stimulating activity in itself.

SAND FOR ALL

Sand play activities are very multipurpose. If the receptacle is large and can be placed on a table, or better still on a floor, then by gathering the group around the tray, this can enhance group work enormously. If, however, this is impossible, then individual group members can have their own personal trays or cups. Sand play can be enjoyed by people in wheelchairs, people in bed, people wherever they are.

If arms or hands cannot be moved, then how about trying feet? A small seed tray is big enough to put a foot into! Imagine how that must feel! We have all had the experience of walking barefoot in the sand. Is it really too much to try and let handicapped people have similar experiences? Ideally of course the tray ought to be big enough to get more than one foot into. It doesn't matter if they don't like it. Once this has been established on their grounds and not ours, then this is OK. It is unforgivable to presume that they won't like it before it has even been tried.

Golden rule — don't ask someone to do something that you are not prepared to do yourself.

Sand does not create the many problems that other activities do. A brush and pan will quickly remove all trace of any mess. However, some sand will stain hands, etc., yellow; sharp sand is best. Like many activities it takes some fore-thought and planning in setting up, and if the group are very profoundly handicapped then there may not be instant results. But this should never put you off. Persevere a little. It's no good complaining that people won't respond if they are not given enough variety and range of activities to respond to. Maybe the only thing that is missing is the sand pit! Can you really afford not to try it?

Working With Clay

Red clay is a very stimulating and flexible medium that can be used with profoundly handicapped groups. It is relatively inexpensive to buy and warrants little storage space. If used wisely it can last for a long period of time. Red clay has a look and feel about it that is really quite primitive. It is very easy to work, and either large or small amounts can be used, depending on the needs and abilities of the individual at the time. It ought to be part of every practitioner's stock of equipment. The greatest advantage that red clay has for me is its flexibility. It can be tailored to suit all needs and all ability levels, therefore making it an accessible activity for everyone, despite the degree of handicap. It can be used in one-to-one work and groups, equally successfully.

For profoundly handicapped people who cannot see, red clay is valuable in that it can be heard and felt. If a little water is added to the clay, the consistency and texture become much softer, but not too runny, and when squeezed in this state, it makes all sorts of strange and wonderful noises.

Almost anything can be done with clay. It can be rolled out flat, or manipulated into different shapes. Patterns can be made on table-tops or paper by holding a piece of clay and just dabbing it on the surface. It is very soothing simply to hold a piece of clay. If left to dry out, then the clay will harden. But this can soon be recycled. Wrap the hard clay in strong polythene and bash it extremely hard. Once in tiny pieces, this can then be mixed with water and eventually worked back to the consistency required. This might not be an activity appropriate to many profoundly handicapped people — because of the inability to lift a hammer, or maybe because of the physical effort involved. However, it is an excellent way of getting rid of pent-up feelings and emotions and is perfect for higher-ability handicapped people, to say nothing of how beneficial it can be for staff!

Clay can be a medium that can bring people closer together. A group project in which all members of the group can contribute to a finished product is an extremely worthwhile activity to undertake. It might not be possible for all group members actually to be seated around the project, but this should not be a problem as the clay can be worked individually, and then added to the group 'sculp' when finished. The important point to make is that everyone can play a part in the group process.

Seeing an end product is very important. True creativity has little to do with 'artistic presentation'. Creativity is within us all, but unless the outlet or facilitator is provided then it will seldom emerge. Red clay can be this facilitator, and it needs to be used to be fully appreciated. In the search for new techniques and stimulatory methods, you don't ever have to look very far to find them.

Back to Nature

I feel that the inclusion of something horticultural is very important in any activity programme, not just for profoundly handicapped groups but for all groups. As with all activities, careful planning and preparation must be accomplished in a way to suit both individual and group needs. It might not be possible to dig over vegetable patches and prune roses, but there are a great many things that can be done within this area that are not only stimulating and educational but also good fun.

GETTING STARTED

Having decided to embark on a gardening activity, the very first thing that needs to be decided upon is the scale of the project. Putting in requisition slips for a 100 metre greenhouse will certainly not assist your case with administrative finance officers. But if your intent is to acquire stimulatory plants and foliage, then almost all equipment needed can be begged and borrowed, or taken on a permanent loan basis.

All keen gardeners have such a passion about their work that they would be only too delighted to share their knowledge, skills, and importantly, tools of the trade with you. But they cannot do any of these things unless they are approached. Their advice is invaluable and needs to be sought before a start is made. It is so important to have the *right* plants, and the right equipment.

Having gathered together the very basics, then canvass family and friends for cuttings. It won't take long to have a small collection on the go. How you go about acquiring containers, display pots and troughs and hanging baskets is very much dependent on how persuasive and persistent you can be!

A SIMPLE GUIDELINE

Lemon-scented geraniums, when touched ever so lightly, leave a very pleasant smell on fingers or clothes.

Freesias are just one variety of small flower that can be grown very successfully from seeds. Their aroma is powerful but pleasing.

Pansies and primulas are small but colourful.

Hyacinths, as with lots of bulbs, are relatively easy to hold, and manageable, and again provide aromatic stimulation.

Cactus plants provide a wealth of tactile stimulation — but must be used with caution.

Cress, onions, beans and carrots plus a jam jar or lid and a piece of blotting paper and some tender loving care will produce very fast results, which can be seen almost daily.

Lilies, amaryllis and other flowers grown from corms and bulbs not only provide magnificent floral displays but can be used year after year, and are stimulating to watch.

Growing tomatoes is not really as overadventurous as it might sound. This can always be done as a little sideline — selling the crop at a competitive price to provide extra funding for the really adventurous elements that you may wish to develop at a later time!

Readers may be interested to know that quite a number of shops and departmental stores in the High Street are often on the look out for places to send their plants when expiry dates have been reached, or when plants are just past their best. They will never send them to your Unit if they are unaware that you want what they have to offer. Without being greedy, this is an excellent way of acquiring extra bits and pieces to add to your already blossoming collection. These plants may not be up to the standards required for fair trading — but they can be an invaluable asset to your new programme. You will get a better response if you can make a personal appearance to present your case. Telephones are too impersonal and don't always allow enough opportunity for your enthusiasm to be conveyed in its true light.

Whatever plants or seeds are chosen, they will all need looking after and nurturing. Someone has to water them and, with larger plants such as Swiss cheese or rubber plants, someone has to clean them; and from time to time, plants need repotting. These are all activities that profoundly handicapped people can be involved in. They don't always necessarily have to *do* a complete task. For example, with repotting, coordination may be difficult but maybe they can be given the opportunity to feel the compost.

Plants and foliage are objects that can be seen and felt. Watching something grow from a tiny seed to a living plant can be very stimulating. Being involved in that process is providing yet another opportunity for being able to do something that is very creative. Creativity is an area that many profoundly handicapped children and adults are deprived from experiencing. But by including a naturistic element in their programme, this can be minimised. I have never thought that it wasn't worth at least a try. Better to know that it is not applicable because it doesn't suit individual needs rather than simply that the practitioner sees it as being too much trouble to undertake.

9   How About ... ?

Outings

Anyone who has organised an outing for a group of profoundly handicapped people will know what a headache it
can be. By the same token, it can bring so much happiness
and enjoyment — the very reasons why outings ought to be
encouraged. Arranging transport, packed lunches, drinks,
wheelchairs and change of clothing are all pegs that can be
easily used to hang all the excuses on for not going.

What happens is that we tend to look at all the peripheral
aspects of the activity. Somehow we don't seem to be able
to envisage how anyone is going to react, because we are so
concerned with how *we* are going to manage wheelchairs and
incontinence. Very often it is much easier not to go. We have
not got the right to decide whether the outing is going to be
enjoyable or not. If our motivation levels for going are very
low, then this will be conveyed to the group we take, resulting in negative attitudes all round. We can't expect anyone
else to enjoy the day if we are unable to.

For many, the only time that they travel is to the Centre
or school and home again. It must come as a welcome surprise
to discover that there are other roads apart from those that
are travelled daily. Change of scenery and change of co-
passengers can be stimulating. A lot of the pleasure gained is
accountable to just the journey.

Trips to the zoo, cinema and theatre are all outings that
should be considered. We are not in any position to decide in
advance that our groups are going to understand/take it all
in/enjoy/benefit from such an activity. Neither can we say
that the reverse will apply. We will have no idea until we try

it. Previous experiences may indicate that the outing may not be all that successful, but we cannot say for certain that this will be the case this time. We have to remember that each experience must be judged on its own performance, and not on those of days gone by. We can afford to make mistakes. Better to know for a fact that James does not like the circus because while he was there he kicked up such a fuss that his dislike was obvious, rather than the situation of never having tried it and not knowing for sure.

A change of pattern and scenery can relieve the boredom of routine. A walk to the local park, or a trip out to far away places — both are valuable. Problems of transport should not put outings 'out of reach'. A visit to the local market or corner shop will be a welcome break. Supermarkets are colourful and lively places, full of new sights and sounds to be experienced.

We come back to the question of standards again. Would we be content to travel the same route to work each day and not have any other opportunities for getting out and about? Of course we would not. So why expect others to be content with it?

Playgrounds can be great fun, especially sound playgrounds. The group may not be able to run up and down the slide, but they may derive a lot of pleasure from watching or hearing others doing it. Outings are activities that present the handicapped person with new surroundings and new experiences — both stimulating aspects that should not be ignored.

Photographs

Photographs are taken to record events and activities. They are pleasurable to look at and are reminders of what we did at a particular time. For the profoundly handicapped person, their uses are many.

Case Study

Janice loves to sit and look through albums. She is never very keen to sit still with other activities but, once her photographs are out, her behaviour changes quite remarkably. Her concentration is good, and she has started to smile in anticipation of the 'next page' when she knows it is full of pictures of her.

James squeals with delight when shown photographs of himself. Unable to speak, he excitedly points to the picture, then points to whoever is featured in it.

Inevitably, in any group there are 'posers'. Christine loves the camera. She rushes in front of it, almost demanding that photos are taken of her. She then adopts model-like postures and waits for the flash.

So, in many ways, taking photographs and looking at the prints can be a very stimulating activity. Apart from the fun involved in actually taking them, there are a number of other ways in which they can be used. Reinforcement of activities and outings that they portray is possible. 'Do you remember?' games can be played. Identification games are another idea — 'Show me the photo of John', 'Who else is in the photo?', and so on.

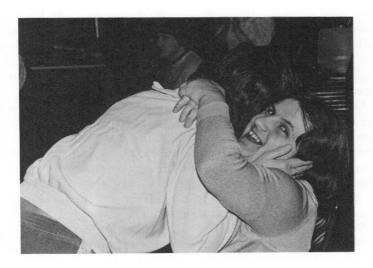

For visitors to the Unit, a display of photographs can not only give immediate information on what people have been doing but can also provide colourful backgrounds to the area that they spend their time in. For parents, they provide proof of how time is spent. For all parties involved they are pleasurable. The value of having photographs should never be underestimated.

Pets

There has been growing interest in recent years as to the importance that pets play in the rehabilitation process following illness, both physical and psychiatric. Patients who are discharged home from hospital, and who have a dog or cat for company, make a more rapid recovery than those patients who do not have pets. Quite a number of professional bodies recognise the importance of 'stroking' and see it as being very therapeutic.

Obviously we all react differently to animals. Some people are dog and cat people, while others are not. I am not advocating that we should surround profoundly handicapped people by pets and just sit back and wait for the cures — but like many things, this is an area that we ought at least to consider. Pets are good company. For all their respective self-sufficiency, they are dependent on their owners for feeding and for caring for them. For all their aloofness, cats do respond very positively to our stroking and will display their pleasure by purring.

Dogs tend to show different character traits. They return our care for them quite demonstrably — overt signs of affection, protectiveness and their obvious love of their master. They respond to our spoken word, sulk when we go out and leave them, and greet us with excitement when we return home. For the blind or deaf person, they can be trained to be their eyes and ears. They provide an independence that would otherwise be unattainable.

Fish are relaxing to watch — almost hypnotic.

Birds, rabbits, mice, hamsters, tortoises and so on are just some of the pets that give children pleasure. The child who grows up in a home where there are pets has not only a better awareness of those animals but also has the opportunity to develop a sense of responsibility, in terms of feeding and caring for them.

Whatever the pet, there are responsibilities involved, and these must not be taken lightly. But there are advantages for the handicapped child in having access to animals. For city children, who do not have the daily contact with livestock that country children have, there is added excitement when they see cows, sheep, goats and so on.

Many zoos now have a 'farm' area, where children are encouraged to have close-up experiences of many animals that country children take for granted. Seeing a picture of a horse and listening to the sound that it makes can never be a substitute for coming into contact with the real thing.

For handicapped children and adults, their worlds are narrowed by so many outside factors, predominantly determined by the attitudes and opinions of those who are in positions of power — the people who care. For the profoundly handicapped person, their very existence warrants effort and energy all the time by others. Everything they do requires the cooperation and help of at least one other person.

I am asking the reader to consider that when we dismiss areas of activity that may be possible, is the criterion because we don't want it or is it really because the handicapped person in our care would not really benefit from it? If animals are accessible for normal children, is there really any justification in them not being accessible to handicapped children?

Story Telling

This is an activity best illustrated by case studies.

Case Study

Sam hated group activities. As soon as the group appeared to settle down to an art session, or baking session, or whatever, his behaviour became very disruptive. We decided not to pressurise him into joining in, but we did want to find a calming activity that could be used to diffuse the inevitability of the outbursts. We found it in stories.

Using his favourite books, one of us sat and read quietly to him — pointing to pictures as we went along and giving him all the encouragement we could for him to indicate characters and objects by name. After a very short period of time, he quite spontaneously started to pick things out on his own.

He now often takes a book from the shelves and reads it with a very different attitude than he did previously. Is it because now he knows the story and therefore has greater interest? Who can say? But his attitude to the other group members has changed. He no longer displays disruptive behaviour in art sessions or any other group activity.

Case Study

Julie would sit for hours on end just rocking backwards and forwards, making the occasional grunting noise. Her attention was hard to attract, and there was certainly little reaction from her whenever she was spoken to. We started to read very short stories, using different levels of intonation to try to make it more stimulating. Before long, she started to get quite excited about it. She rocked furiously whenever we got the books ready, and started to giggle quite uncontrollably. During the story, she stopped rocking, and even though it only lasted for a few minutes at a time, she looked almost relaxed.

When the time for stories was over, she reverted back to her rocking, turning her face away from the group, and nearly always sitting with her face to the wall. We repeated stories, and she soon started to recognise 'what was coming next'. Gradually she started to look at the pictures and slowly started to identify certain characters and objects. There was never any degree of consistency with this, but she nevertheless started to respond in a very positive way.

In both instances, there was a noticeable difference in both behaviour and use of speech. Story telling is a very calming and soothing activity. Depending upon the story of course, it can also be exciting and noisy! But it is an ideal activity to use on a one-to-one basis, and also as a group activity. It really does not matter that the end of the story is known — what is important is the time that is given to telling it.

One of the difficulties in working with profoundly handicapped people is the ability to be able to relate 'outside' skills and activities to their own environment and within their own capabilities. You really cannot expect to get a reaction from a picture of a dragon if there is no information given about dragons. We must ever be aware of the fact that there are a multitude of accessible words within the language that we use — but we can never assume the same accessibility applies to the handicapped people we work alongside. It is our responsibility to introduce these new words in a way that is easy and comprehensible.

Using picture books with interesting stories is one of the ways in which we can do this. Another way is to make up our own stories. This does not have to be a complicated task. Something very simple will suffice:

There was a young man called David, who liked to watch the TV and listen to his records. One day when the sun decided not to shine and the big rain clouds poured lots of water on his garden, he thought that he would listen to some music.

The cat/dog/rabbit/budgie thought that this would be a good idea too. So they all settled down in David's room for a quiet afternoon . . . and so on.

Once again, we come back to the question of our own resources. We must not always expect the activities to be handed to us on a plate. There are times when we have to look to ourselves for them. This can be one of those times. A balanced day should include time spent not only on movement and boisterous activity but also on quiet activities. Telling stories can always be a happy medium.

Massage

Profoundly handicapped people are as readily susceptible to tension as anyone else. There are a variety of techniques that can be used to relieve tension. One that is easily accessible is massage. Apart from being a facilitator for close physical contact, it can be an extremely enjoyable activity if used appropriately and sensibly.

Gently massaging or stroking known tension areas, such as neck and shoulders, is soothing and relaxing. Irrespective of the degree of handicap, massage can be applied in almost any position. Hands and feet should not be forgotten as being areas that can be easily stroked. Massage is an activity that does not need any equipment. It can also be done most effectively without having to undress people.

If areas of skin are dry, then rubbing in hand cream will not only relieve this but is also a very soothing sensation.

We know ourselves how we feel when we get all tensed up about something, and how relaxing it can be to have someone just gently rub the back of our neck or stroke our forehead. I have found it very useful as a means of developing new relationships with profoundly handicapped people — apart from the very obvious advantages of including it in an activity programme.

Volunteers

It can be very frustrating when you want to do something and you can't because there are not enough pairs of hands to put the idea into practice. Having an extra pair of hands does not always solve the problem. You can have the highest staffing ratios imaginable but, unless the calibre of help is right, the extra staffing will make little, if any, difference.

There are voluntary organisations operating in all areas. Between them they have a wealth of skills that will be of tremendous value — it is just a question of finding out who they are, where they are, and how their skills can be best employed to help your situation. Rarely will the extra help just fall into your lap. You have to explain your situation, so that the agency has a clear picture of what is needed. This will enable them to find the right person or people to help you. Being vague and presenting a plea for just extra pairs of hands is not enough.

A positive and enthusiastic approach is what is needed. The other important point to make is that all efforts must be made to ensure that you do not appear to be greedy. It might be too much to request help for an entire morning, afternoon or evening. A little help can often be far more valuable than a three-hour stint. Work out exactly what it is that you need help for. Try not to be dishonest. If the helper will be expected to spoon-feed while they are there, then this sort of information ought to be known to them in advance. Waiting until they arrive on their first day and then springing it on them might easily lead them to change their minds, and withdraw entirely. Sensible allocation of duties is called for. Start with just one hour, and then see how the time is increased — on their instigation not yours.

Volunteers can be of tremendous benefit to any organisation, but it has to be remembered that they are volunteers. Having a regular commitment from someone to read stories for half an hour enables the activity to be timetabled and planned. Having volunteers to take part in, and direct, activities increases staffing levels. Every little helps, and although it would be marvellous to think that volunteers were not needed, this is impracticable and unrealistic. There can never be enough pairs of hands. Let's face it, the authorities are never going to provide us with staffing levels that we think are appropriate, so calling on the help of volunteers is a sensible move to make. Whether they are reading stories, helping in group sessions, washing hair or just being with people, they all have an extremely valuable part to play.

During the endless discussions that always seem to be going on with regard to arguments for and against raised staffing levels, the authorities can never back down to footing the bill for an advert in the local paper. From their standpoint, it is much more cost effective to pay for an advert as opposed to paying for another member of staff. But they are hardly likely to think of it themselves, so you must bring it to their attention — tactfully, of course!

10   The Final Word

Out of Space

Shortly before completing this manuscript I was asked by a senior administrator to write a short list of what I felt was needed should the Unit be moved to another location. My list almost read like another book!

Very high on the priority scale was accommodation. If there is variety of environment then this in itself can be stimulating. Eating, drinking, working, playing all in the same room is dull. Far more than one room is required, though some practitioners would feel that any room would suffice. But I feel it must be said that it won't suffice at all — not if progress is going to be made. One room might be all right if what is expected is a baby-sitting service, but not if expectations are higher. It really isn't a case of a bad workman blaming his tools. It is a question of not being satisfied with forever having to make do when it comes to making provision for profoundly mentally handicapped people. This very much forgotten and lost group of people in care settings end up having whatever other groups do not want.

If Special Care Units are providing a good service, and have the right pieces of equipment to assist them in doing just that, then this will need space — and lots of it. Cramped conditions are irritating. Without the room to move around, then exploration is limited. Messy activities should be done in messy rooms, quiet activities should be done in quiet rooms, so that the activities can be related to the area of work.

The level of comprehension or degree of handicap is important. For practitioners and families working towards widening horizons and bringing new experiences to the profoundly handicapped person, every situation is a learning situation. Stimulus should be all around, not just the sort of stimulus that comes from chiming mobiles, or bright pictures on walls, or auditory stimulus, but the peaceful stimulus of pastel shades in designated quiet areas.

The environment for the profoundly handicapped child or adult is very small. For the vast majority, their environment changes little in a lifetime. Taking some effort in providing surroundings which are conducive to learning and progress being made is surely not asking too much — or is it?

Conclusion

Throughout the writing of this book, I have become increasingly aware of just how isolated the handicapped world still is — for those who work in it, but most especially for those who suffer from it. Isolation breeds isolation, and practitioners unfortunately are the worst perpetuators of this. The hardest task is not to do what we do but to inform others of what we are doing.

Unless involved in handicap in some way, the vast majority of the population see only one side of handicap — that of horror stories and enquiries. I would never advocate a cover up — but this type of reporting does tend to tar everyone with the same brush. But we cannot condemn the media for bad publicity when this is the only side of handicap they ever get to hear about. It would be unrealistic to deny that this side of handicap exists — but it isn't the only side. We must decide what we are going to do about it. Either we remain in our cocoons of isolation with our heads stuck in the sand, or we do something constructive and positive about exposing the sides of handicap that need to be exposed if they are ever going to be understood. If enough people get together, jump up and down and shout about it often and long enough, then eventually another side of handicap will emerge. It will be from this side that the support and the understanding still very much needed will be forthcoming.

The media can play a very important role in all this — but only if they are aware of it, and not isolated from it. If we value what we are doing, then we are going to want to tell the world about it. We rarely hesitate to complain about handicap, so why do we hold back from shouting about all the good things that are going on? And there are so many good and exciting things happening all the time. By not sharing our valuable experiences, we are contributing to the isolation, reinforcing a negative press and preventing a widening of horizons for the general public. Ultimately this is doing very little to change the misguided attitudes that still prevail. Good media coverage isn't going to cure handicap, but it could provoke public and political opinion into finding the resources for more research and improving facilities. *We* must take on some of this responsibility.

The excitement and anticipation of finding the answers to unresolved problems will not be inhibited by an increase in resources. We have waited long enough to get this far. If we could share a little bit more, this might prompt others to share their feelings and experiences so that any barriers still left standing would be insignificant and unimportant.

We must all of us hope that one day, in the not too distant future, we really will have a good base on which we can build the better future that is long awaited and God knows so long overdue for our handicapped friends.

Appendix 1:
Interesting Reading

American Red Cross (1977). *Adapted Aquatics*, Doubleday.
Association of Swimming Therapy (1981). *Swimming for the Disabled*, E. P. Publishing.
Furneaux, B. (1969). *The Special Child*, Pelican, Third Edition, 1981.
Further Education Unit (1984). *Learning for Independence*, eds A. Dean and S. Hegarty, Chameleon Press.
Goodridge, J. (1970). *Drama in the Primary School*, Heinemann Educational Books.
Hogg, J. and Sebba, J. (1986). *Profound Retardation and Multiple Impairment: A Developmental and Educational Approach*, Croom Helm.
Jennings, S. (1978). *Remedial Drama*, Pitman, and A. & C. Black.
Jennings, S. (ed.) (1983). *Creative Therapy*, Kemble.
Levete, G. (1982). *No Handicap to Dance*, Souvenir Press.
McClintock, A. (1984). *Drama for Mentally Handicapped Children*, Souvenir Press.
Mittler, P. (1979). *People Not Patients*, Methuen.
Oswin, M. (1984). *They Keep Going Away: Critical Study of Short Term Residential Care Services for Children Who Are Mentally Handicapped*, Oxford University Press.
Pavey, D. (1979). *Art Based Games*, Methuen.
Potterfield, J. (1978). *Profoundly handicapped adults can do much more*. Report of a research study. *Teaching & Training*, **16**, 3–10 (Souvenir Press, Human Horizons Series).

Scher, A. and Verrall, C. (1975). *100+ Ideas for Drama*, Heinemann Educational Books.

Segal, S. S. (1974). *No Child Is Ineducable*, Pergamon, Second Edition.

Segal, S. S. (1984). *Society and Mental Handicap: Are We Ineducable?*, D. J. Costello.

Shearer, A. (1981). *Bringing Mentally Handicapped Children Out of Hospital*, Kings Fund Paper.

Stevens, M. (1976). *The Educational and Social Needs of Children With Severe Handicap*, Edward Arnold, Second Edition.

Swann, W. (ed.) (1981). *The Practice of Special Education*, Basil Blackwell in association with the Open University Press.

Tomlinson, R. (1982). *Disability, Theatre and Education*, Souvenir Press.

Wing, L. (ed.) (1980). *Austistic Children: A Guide for Parents*, Constable, Third Edition.

Wing, L. (ed.) (1982). *Early Childhood Autism: Clinical, Educational and Social Aspects*, Pergamon Press, Second Edition.

Appendix 2:
Useful Addresses

Association for All Speech Impaired Children (AFASIC), 347 Central Markets, Smithfield, London EC1A 9NH

Association of Dance Movement Therapy, 99 South Hill Park, London NW3 2SP

Association of Parents of Vaccine Damaged Children, 2 Church Street, Shipton-on-Stour, Warwick CV36 4AP

Association for Spina Bifida and Hydrocephalus (ASBAH), 22 Upper Woburn Place, London WC1H 0EP

British Agencies for Adoption and Fostering, 121–123 Camberwell Road, London SE25

British Association of Art Therapy, 13c Northwood Road, London N6 5TL

British Association for Dramatherapists, P.O. Box 98, Kirbymoorside, York YO6 6EX

British Association of Music Therapy, Harperbury Hospital, Harper Lane, Shenley, Radlett, Herts WD7 9HQ

British Institute of Mental Handicap, Wolverhampton Road, Kidderminster, Worcestershire DY10 3PP

Campaign for Mentally Handicapped People (CMH), 12a Maddox Street, London W1R 9PL

Castle Priory, Thames Street, Wallingford, Oxon OX10 0HE

Citizens Advice Bureaux. Refer to your local area.

Contact a Family, 16 Strutton Ground, London SW1

Department of Education and Science (DES), Elizabeth House, York Road, London SE1 7PH

Department of Health and Social Security (DHSS), Alexander Fleming House, Elephant & Castle, London SE1 6BY

Disabled Living Foundation, 380–384 Harrow Road, London W9 2HU

Down's Children's Association, 4 Oxford Street, London W1

Dramatherapy Consultants, 6 Nelsons Avenue, St Albans, Hertfordshire AL1 5RY

Further Education Unit (FEU), Department of Education and Science, Honeypot Lane, Canons Park, Stanmore, Middlesex HA7 1AZ

Hester Adrian Research Centre, The University, Manchester M13 9PL

International Cerebral Palsy Society, 5a Netherhall Gardens, London NW3 5RN

The Kings Fund Centre, Albert Street, London NW1 7NE

Kith and Kids, 27 Old Park Ridings, Grange Park, London N21 2EX

National Association of Mental Health (MIND), 22 Harley Street, London W1

National Association of Swimming Clubs for the Handicapped, 219 Preston Grove, Brighton, Sussex BN1 6FL

National Autistic Society, 276 Willesden Lane, London NW2 5RB

National Children's Bureau, 8 Wakely Street, Islington, London EC1V 7QE

National Council of Civil Liberties (NCCL), 21 Tabard Street, London SE1 4LA

National Deaf-Blind and Rubella Association (SENSE), 311 Grays Inn Road, London WC1X 8PT

National Deaf Children's Society, 45 Hereford Road, London W2 5AH

National Elfrida Rathbone Society, 11a Whitworth Street, Manchester M1 3GW

National Society for Epilepsy, Chalfont St Peter, Bucks SL9 0RJ

National Society for Prevention of Cruelty to Children (NSPCC), 67 Saffron Hill, London EC1N 8RS

Royal National Institute for the Blind (RNIB), 224 Great Portland Street, London W1N 6AA

Royal Society for Mentally Handicapped Children and Adults, 123 Golden Lane, London EC1Y 0RT

The Spastics Society, 12 Park Crescent, London W1N 4EQ

Appendix 3:
The Profound Retardation and Multiple Handicap Project

'This is an important reference point for all practitioners and parents. Their address is:

The Profound Retardation and Multiple Handicap Project,
Piper Hill School,
200 Yew Tree Lane,
Northenden,
Manchester M23 0FF
Tel: 061-998 4161

This project, set up by MENCAP in response to pressure from parents and practitioners, should go some way towards meeting the needs of PRMH people, their families, and all those working with this population. The project has the support of the Hester Adrian Research Centre at Manchester University, which will assist in the evaluation of the project.

Initially, information is being collated on the education and care of profoundly retarded and multiple handicapped children and adults. Using the information from surveys carried out nationally and from published sources and consultations with practitioners and families, an information resource bank will be established.

By reviewing models of practice, identifying and initiating methods of stimulation and education, the project envisages providing information that will assist maximum development for profoundly and multiple handicapped children and adults.

Workshops will be set up for parents and practitioners, tailor-made to suit family needs.'

This is something that will at last bring together an overview of exactly what is happening nationally in the field of profound mental handicap.

Hopefully, the project will attract further funding to go beyond the two-year limit. Now that we all have a central source and resource bank, we not only have the responsibility to use this information for benefit but we also have the opportunity to contribute our own experiences and skills towards making it grow. I can only urge readers to contact the project administrator at the above address for further information.

Appendix 4:
Reference Reading for Historical Background

An interesting read for research into the historical background, but by no means exhaustive.

Bayley, M. (1973). *Mental Handicap and Community Care*, Routledge and Kegan Paul.

Bluglass, R. (1983). *A Guide to the Mental Health Act 1983*, Churchill Livingstone.

DES (1978). *Special Educational Needs*, Report of the Committee of Enquiry into the Education of Handicapped Children and Young People, Chairman Mrs. M. Warnock, Cmnd 7212, HMSO.

DHSS (1971). *Better Services for the Mentally Handicapped*, Cmnd 4683, HMSO.

DHSS (1976). *Fit for the Future*, Report of the Committee on Child Health Services, Chairman Professor S. D. M. Court, Cmnd 6684, HMSO.

Furneaux, B. (1969). *The Special Child*, Pelican, Third Edition, 1981.

Hoenig, J. and Hamilton, M. H. (1969). *The Desegregation of the Mentally Ill*, Routledge and Kegan Paul.

Hunter, R. A. and McAlpine, I. (1963). *Three Hundred Years of Psychiatry*, Oxford University Press.

Jones, K. (1960). *Mental Health and Social Policy 1845–1959*, Routledge and Kegan Paul.

Jones K. (1972). *A History of the Mental Health Services*, Routledge and Kegan Paul.

Mittler, P. (1979). *People Not Patients*, Methuen.

National Council for Civil Liberties (1950). *50 000 Outside the Law*, London.

Office of Population Censuses and Surveys (1979). *Nurses and Residential Social Workers Caring for the Mentally Handicapped*, Report of the Committee of Enquiry into Nursing and Care of the Mentally Handicapped, Chairman Mrs P. Jay, HMSO.

Pritchard, D. G. (1963). *Education and the Handicapped 1760–1960*, Routledge and Kegan Paul.

Royal Commission on the Law Relating to Mental Illness and Mental Deficiency 1954–1957 (1957). Chairman Lord Percy, Cmnd 169, HMSO.

Royal Commission on the Care and Control of the Feeble Minded 1904–1908 (1908). Chairman Lord Radnor, Cd 4202, HMSO.

Swann, W. (ed.) (1981). *The Practice of Special Education*, Basil Blackwell in association with the Open University Press.

The School Health Service 1908–1974 (1975). HMSO.

Wood Report (1929). Report of the Mental Deficiency Committee, Being a Joint Committee of the Board of Education and the Board of Control, HMSO.